ICONS

il2d. 110
Image Movers Digital. 111
Infinite Scale Design Group 112
janek's favourites. 113
Jesús Vilamajó. 114
john st. 115
Jozias Dawson 116
JSK Dipl. Ing. Architekten. . . . 117
Julie Bayard. 118
LaLuca Comunicacion 119
L'Âmoscope. 120
Leeuwenkamp Architects 121
Legend 122
Levy LLC 123
Lindsey Wade Photography 124
Mad Design 125
MALER HIMMELDIRK 126
mediaBOOM 127
Medusateam 128
Metropolis 129
Mkt Virtual 130
MOA 131
modelplus 132
Morgan Archive 133
Mr. Taylor. 134
multimediaHAAM. 135
Mutabor 136
My Poor Brain 137
nanozoom 138
National Television 139
Nayef Francis 140
Neumann Health 141
New Deal Studio 142
Objeto de Desejo 143
Openfield Creative. 144
Optiker Krauss 145
Prospect Denim 146
Quik Cia. de Dança 147
Revolver Creative 148
Robin Skjoldborg 149
Ruud Baan. 150

RVLT 151
Saants DI 152
Santa Produtora 153
Saso Kos Photography 154
Scratch Music Group 155
Secret Circus 156
SectionSeven 157
Serge De Marre 158
Sir Patroclo. 159
SKAFFS 160
Som de Lisboa 161
Sonar 162
Square Circle 163
Stereo 164
Stereonoise 165
SUBRAUMSTUDIO 166
TAKAKI KUMADA 167
TBWA\Toronto. 168
Technical Design Studio 169
Teri Studios. 170
The Cuban Brothers 171
Transtorna. 172
Troika. 173
Tronic Studio 174
Uniform 175
Urbansoldierz 176
VaryWell 177
Veneno 178
Vermeersch 179
Vincent Vella 180
Virtual Murder 181
W3Haus 182
Wat doet Howard.nu 183
Weblounge 184
WHITEvoid 185
XN Brand Dynamics 186
YAMA 187
yolk 188
Zero Style. 189
CREDITS 190
IMPRINT 191

The Power of Online Portfolios
Steve Le Marquand

At Resn, we believe that online portfolios are now an essential tool for presenting creative work to prospective clients and industry peers. Gone are the times when portfolios were carefully packed up into protective packaging and given to a clumsy courier only to arrive bent more than a taxi's fender. The creative industry has a strong association with the Internet which has developed as a forum and incubator for creative culture. Much creative notoriety can be gained via the Internet owing to the provision of uninhibited peer review. With a creative presence on the Internet your portfolios can achieve immense visibility.

We'd have to throw it out there that the growing popularity of online portfolios can be attributed to creative individuals seeking work over larger geographical distances but requiring a cost-effective method for delivery of their presentations. Yes, times have changed.

Engaging the audience of your portfolio is extremely important today as your portfolio competes for attention amongst other vibrant interactive media. But do not fret. With an online portfolio you can mutate your audience from viewers into users with online's ability to present truly interactive content. As most of you will know, Adobe's Flash allows for the online portfolios of today to showcase various forms of work including video, audio and interactive. The development of technology like this creates a flexible platform for the presentation of a modern and truly experiential portfolio of work. At Resn we designed our main website with a portfolio style structure that focuses on presenting our work in a clean and dynamic fashion. It is better to let your work speak for itself!

Online portfolios are infinitely updateable in comparison with standard physical portfolios which provide little functionality for revision of your ever-developing creative arsenal. Think about how many outdated portfolios are lying around offices gathering dust! These obsolete portfolios could actually damage your creative profile if someone was to pick one up and believe that your work from five years ago is what you are doing today.

Measurability is one of the most definable benefits of an online portfolio that we see at Resn. Incorporating standard website statistical software into your online portfolio will easily illustrate what content is of interest to the general audience and how the dynamics of your portfolio are functioning. This statistical feedback allows the portfolio to have its structure revised and updated effectively to optimise its functionality. Portfolio stats are also great for ego inflation or the pure indulgence of voyeurism.

The scalability of portfolios presented online provides functionality not found in a physical format. Online portfolio content is not restricted by the physical limitations associated with traditional paperweight portfolios. A portfolio book, for example, may have thirty pages of content whereas an online portfolio may contain an unlimited amount of work. That doesn't mean going and boring the poor recipient with everything you have worked on for the last 10 years! Be selective in your choice of work for your online portfolio and treat the experience of it as you would a hard-copy portfolio.

Now it has to be said that online portfolios benefit the environment. It's true! They help reduce energy wasted during the transport of physical portfolios to their recipients and materials used in their production. This may seem like a little thing to some of you but even if you don't care about protecting the environment, your prospective client or employer may do.

With the use of the Internet you can easily achieve efficient distribution of your online portfolio. Physical portfolio distribution is hindered by the constraints of its physical form. Getting your portfolio to your audience in a prompt and cost-effective manner is essential in a modern world where the international audience is just as important as the local one. You may just get that job because your portfolio arrived that day via email compared with others which are still sitting in the courier's van while he eats his lunch. It is a fast-paced world and sometimes speed will get you results over tradition.

We find at Resn that a lot of designers, artists, or developers we have working with us are ones we have found via word of mouth, either through the Internet from our trawling of portfolio sites or from industry peers passing us web links. Never underestimate the power of viral promotion or word-of-mouth marketing. Traditional hard-copy portfolios are difficult for third parties to pass on to other interested parties and this therefore prohibits the portfolio's ability to market itself by word of mouth.

It is never too late. Get your portfolio online today or if you're busy, tomorrow.

Steve Le Marquand is the managing director of **Resn**, an award-winning interactive agency based in Wellington, New Zealand. Over the last years, Resn has been able to create numerous campaigns integrating traditional and new media, winning awards such as The Favourite Website Award, Pixel Awards, The Create Award, the Hot Shop Awards, Netdivers, and SXSW, among many others. <www.resn.co.nz>

Die Macht des Online-Portfolios
Steve Le Marquand

Wir bei Resn glauben, dass Online-Portfolios inzwischen unverzichtbar sind, um potenziellen Kunden und Partnern die Arbeit kreativer Designer zu präsentieren. Vorbei sind die Zeiten, als Portfolios noch sorgfältig und mühevoll verpackt ungeschickten Kurieren übergeben wurden, um schließlich verbogener als die Stoßstange eines Taxis beim Kunden anzukommen. Kreatives Grafikdesign ist eng mit dem Internet verbunden, das zugleich Forum und Brutstätte der Kreativkultur ist. Im Internet kann man dank ungehemmter kollegialer Beurteilung Aufmerksamkeit erregen, und online gestellte Portfolios erreichen einen ungeheuren Verbreitungsgrad.

Die zunehmende Beliebtheit von Online-Portfolios hängt offensichtlich damit zusammen, dass kreative Individuen heutzutage weltweit nach Auftraggebern suchen und eine kosteneffektive Methode brauchen, um ihre Portfolios an den Kunden zu bringen. Ja, die Zeiten haben sich geändert.

Ihr Portfolio muss die Aufmerksamkeit des Betrachters fesseln und steht dabei in Konkurrenz mit anderen interaktiven Medien. Aber keine Sorge, mit einem Online-Portfolio verwandeln Sie durch den Einsatz interaktiver Inhalte Betrachter in Benutzer. Wie den meisten von Ihnen wahrscheinlich bekannt ist, lassen sich mit Flash von Adobe unterschiedliche Projektformen darstellen, auch Video-, Audio- und interaktive Arbeiten. Durch moderne Technologien ist eine flexible Plattform entstanden, auf der zeitgemäße und experimentelle Portfolios präsentiert werden. Unsere Website stellt die Projekte von Resn klar und dynamisch vor. Am besten lässt man die Projekte selbst für sich sprechen!

Im Gegensatz zu herkömmlichen Portfolios lassen sich Online-Portfolios unbegrenzt aktualisieren und an Ihr sich ständig erweiterndes kreatives Spektrum anpassen. Man denke nur daran, wie viele alte Portfolio-Mappen in Büros langsam zustauben! Sie könnten sogar Ihr Kreativprofil beschädigen, falls jemand eines Tages ein fünf Jahre altes Portfolio in die Hände bekäme und es für aktuell hielte.

Messbarkeit ist einer der offensichtlichsten Vorzüge eines Online-Portfolios, die wir bei Resn erkennen können. Durch Verwendung einer Standardsoftware für Websitestatistik lässt sich ermitteln, welche Inhalte die Benutzer am meisten interessieren und wie die Dynamik des Portfolios funktioniert. Anhand des statistischen Feedbacks kann die Struktur des Portfolios überarbeitet und seine Funktionalität optimiert werden. Portfolio-Statistiken sind außerdem gut für den Aufbau überdimensionaler Egos und die Befriedigung voyeuristischer Gelüste.

Die Skalierbarkeit des Online-Portfolios ist ein weiterer unschlagbarer Vorteil gegenüber den physischen Grenzen des alten Formats. Ein Portfolio-Buch hat vielleicht nur 30 Seiten, während ein Online-Portfolio unbegrenzt viele Arbeiten zeigen kann. Das sollte Sie jedoch nicht dazu verleiten, den armen Besucher mit sämtlichen Projekten der vergangenen zehn Jahre zu langweilen! Treffen Sie eine Auswahl, die genauso sorgfältig ist, als handele es sich um ein Hardcopy-Portfolio.

Unbedingt erwähnt werden sollte auch, dass Online-Portfolios umweltfreundlich sind. Hier sparen Sie Material sowie die Energie, die der Transport zum Kunden verbraucht. Das mag manchem nebensächlich erscheinen, doch auch wenn Ihnen Umweltschutz nicht so wichtig ist, könnte er potenziellen Kunden oder Arbeitgebern doch am Herzen liegen.

Es ist wesentlich leichter, ein Online-Portfolio zu verbreiten als ein physisches Portfolio. In der heutigen

www.resn.co.nz

globalisierten Welt, in der internationale Kunden genauso wichtig sind wie nationale oder lokale, ist dies ein entscheidender Vorteil. Sie erhalten den Zuschlag für einen Auftrag vielleicht nur, weil Ihr Portfolio noch am selben Tag per E-Mail ankommt, während die Mappen Ihrer Konkurrenten noch im Auto des Kuriers liegen, der gerade Mittagspause macht. Unsere Welt ist schnell geworden, und Geschwindigkeit bringt manchmal Wettbewerbsvorteile.

Viele der Designer, Illustratoren oder Programmierer, mit denen wir bei Resn arbeiten, haben wir durch Empfehlungen und Verweise gefunden – entweder beim Sichten von Portfolio-Sites im Internet oder durch Weblinks, die von Kollegen verschickt wurden. Unterschätzen Sie nie die Macht von viraler PR oder des mündlichen Marketings. Traditionelle Hardcopy-Portfolios können nicht so leicht weitergegeben werden, was die Verbreitung per Empfehlung stark einschränkt.

Es ist nie zu spät: Stellen Sie Ihr Portfolio noch heute online. Oder – wenn Sie viel zu tun haben – spätestens morgen.

Steve Le Marquand ist Managing Director von **Resn**, einer vielfach ausgezeichneten Interaktiv-Agentur aus Wellington, Neuseeland. Im Laufe der letzten Jahre hat Resn viele Werbekampagnen entwickelt, die traditionelle und neue Medien verbinden. Die Agentur hat zahlreiche Auszeichnungen gewonnen, darunter den Favourite Website Award, Pixel Awards, Create Award, Hot Shop Awards, Netdivers und SXSW. <www.resn.co.nz>

Le pouvoir des sites web de portfolio

Steve Le Marquand

Chez Resn, nous pensons que les sites web de portfolio sont devenus un instrument essentiel pour présenter les projets créatifs aux clients potentiels et aux pairs du secteur. L'heure n'est plus aux portfolios soigneusement emballés dans du papier bulle et confiés à un coursier maladroit, qui arrivent à destination plus froissés que le pare-chocs d'un taxi. Le secteur de la créativité est très lié à Internet, qui est devenu un forum et un incubateur de la culture de la création. Internet peut faire gagner beaucoup de notoriété grâce à un système d'évaluation par les pairs débarrassé de toute inhibition. Et un site web peut donner à votre portfolio une visibilité immense.

On peut supposer que la popularité croissante des portfolios sur Internet est due à des créateurs individuels qui recherchent du travail aux quatre coins du globe mais ont besoin d'une méthode économique pour faire leurs présentations. Oui, les temps ont changé.

Aujourd'hui il est important que votre portfolio réussisse à séduire votre public, car il est concurrencé par d'autres supports interactifs pleins de vitalité. Mais ne vous en faites pas. Avec votre site-portfolio, vous pouvez transformer vos visiteurs en utilisateurs, car sur Internet vous pouvez leur présenter des contenus véritablement interactifs. Comme vous le savez sans doute, Adobe Flash permet de présenter les portfolios sous plusieurs formes, notamment la vidéo et l'audio, et d'y ajouter de l'interactivité. Ce type de technologie crée une plateforme flexible pour présenter un portfolio moderne qui fera vivre à votre public une véritable expérience. Chez Resn, nous avons donné à notre site web principal une structure de portfolio qui se concentre sur la présentation de notre travail avec clarté et dynamisme. Il vaut mieux laisser votre travail parler de lui-même !

Les sites-portfolios sont actualisables à l'infini en comparaison avec les portfolios classiques sur papier, qui n'ont rien de pratique pour réviser votre arsenal créatif en constante évolution. Essayez d'imaginer le nombre de portfolios obsolètes qui sont en train de prendre la poussière en ce moment même ! Un portfolio obsolète pourrait d'ailleurs vous faire du tort si quelqu'un l'ouvrait et pensait que votre travail d'il y a cinq ans reflète ce que vous faites aujourd'hui.

Un portfolio en ligne permet une évaluation précise et actuelle, et pour Resn c'est son avantage le plus concret. En ajoutant à votre portfolio les outils statistiques de tout site web standard, il vous sera facile d'identifier les parties qui intéressent le plus le public en général, et de comprendre comment votre portfolio est utilisé. Ces informations statistiques permettent de réviser et d'actualiser le portfolio efficacement pour en optimiser la fonctionnalité. Elles seront aussi parfaites pour gonfler votre égo, ou pour vous adonner aux plaisirs du voyeurisme.

L'évolutivité des portfolios présentés sur Internet autorise des utilisations que le monde réel ne connaît pas. Leurs contenus ne sont pas soumis aux limites physiques imposées par les portfolios traditionnels en papier. Une version papier peut avoir une trentaine de pages, par exemple, alors qu'une version en ligne peut avoir une quantité de contenus illimitée. Cela ne veut pas dire qu'il faut submerger votre cible avec tout ce que vous avez fait ces dix dernières années ! Soyez sélectif, et pensez à l'expérience qu'en aura votre client, tout comme vous le feriez pour un portfolio sur papier.

Il faut également dire que les sites de portfolio font du bien à l'environnement. C'est vrai ! Ils contribuent à réduire l'énergie gaspillée durant le transport des

portfolios physiques et pour les matériaux utilisés
dans leur production. Cela peut sembler insignifiant
à certains, mais même si la protection de l'environnement ne vous intéresse pas, cela peut intéresser votre
client ou votre patron.

Avec Internet vous n'aurez aucun mal à distribuer
efficacement votre portfolio, alors que la distribution
des versions sur papier est entravée par leur forme
physique. Il est essentiel de faire arriver votre
portfolio à votre client rapidement et économique-
ment, et aujourd'hui le public international est tout
aussi important que le public local. Vous pourriez
très bien décrocher un travail simplement parce que
votre portfolio est arrivé tel jour par e-mail alors
que ceux de vos concurrents attendaient dans la
camionnette du livreur pendant sa pause déjeuner.
Notre monde bouge vite, et parfois c'est la vitesse
qui vous donnera des résultats, davantage que la
tradition.

Chez Resn, nous constatons que beaucoup des
graphistes, artistes ou développeurs avec qui nous
avons travaillé sont des gens que nous avons trouvé
soit par le bouche-à-oreille, soit à travers Internet
en feuilletant des sites de portfolio ou grâce à des
liens que des collègues nous avaient envoyés. Ne sous-
estimez jamais le pouvoir de la promotion virale ou
du bouche-à-oreille. Les portfolios sur papier sont
difficiles à faire passer d'une personne à l'autre, et
cela leur ferme les possibilités du bouche-à-oreille.

Il n'est jamais trop tard. Mettez votre portfolio
sur Internet dès aujourd'hui. Ou si vous êtes occupé,
faites-le demain.

Steve Le Marquand est le directeur administratif de **Resn**, une
agence interactive primée basée à Wellington, en Nouvelle-Zélande.
Ces dernières années, Resn a créé de nombreuses campagnes qui
intègrent les nouveaux médias et les médias traditionnels et a
remporté de nombreuses récompenses, notamment le prix Favourite
Website, le prix Pixel, le prix Create, le prix Hot Shop, Netdivers et
SXSW. <www.resn.co.nz>

Resn
GET A BETTER WORKER
WEBSITE FOR RICOH

- VISIT SITE

Client:
Ricoh Australia

Agency:
Remo Junior Sydney

Resn:
Design, Animation, Development

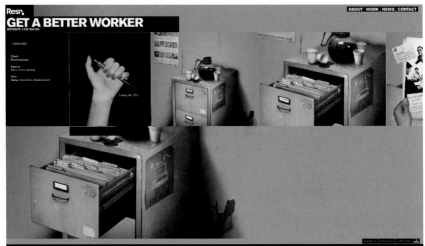

Resn
KISS OFF
GAME FOR NOT OUR FUTURE

- PLAY GAME

Client:
Smokefree New Zealand

Agency:
Resn

Resn:
Creative, Design, Illustration, Animation, Development, Audio

Results:
Played over 1,000,000 times globally in 1 month.

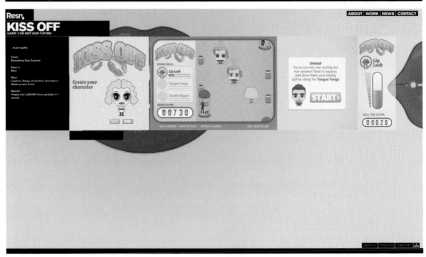

Resn
MINUIT
FEATURING WEBSITE, GAME & ONTECH

GET A BETTER WORKER
KISS OFF
LUKE BUDA
OXYRIDE
MITSUBISHI MOTORS
MOTION REEL

Resn
MINUIT
WEBSITE FOR RESN

www.resn.co.nz

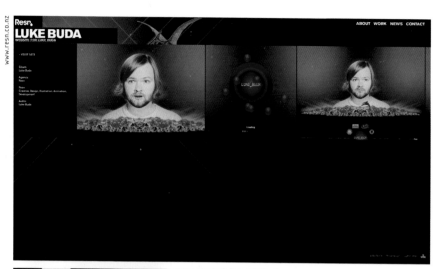

Resn.
LUKE BUDA
WEBSITE FOR LUKE BUDA

ABOUT WORK NEWS CONTACT

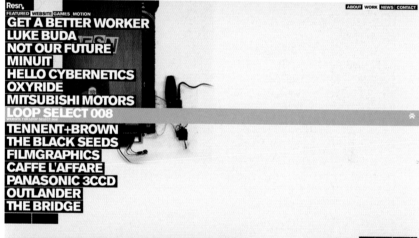

Resn.
FEATURED WEBSITE GAMES MOTION

ABOUT WORK NEWS CONTACT

GET A BETTER WORKER
LUKE BUDA
NOT OUR FUTURE
MINUIT
HELLO CYBERNETICS
OXYRIDE
MITSUBISHI MOTORS
LOOP SELECT 008
WEBSITE FOR LOOP SELECT 008
TENNENT+BROWN
THE BLACK SEEDS
FILMGRAPHICS
CAFFE L'AFFARE
PANASONIC 3CCD
OUTLANDER
THE BRIDGE

Resn.
THE BLACK SEEDS

ABOUT WORK NEWS CONTACT

Resn.
MITSUBISHI MOTORS

ABOUT WORK NEWS CONTACT

Portfolio Redesign
Myles McGuinness

A creative-driven branding company, 9Myles delivers innovative communications that connect people with brands. We drive awareness, build loyalty, and influence perception by discovering the unique ideas that accelerate your business. 9Myles delivers innovative solutions and breakthrough ideas in the areas of brand development, corporate identity, advertising, packaging, website design, events, and product design.

The old website: the problems to be solved

Our previous website was completely Flash-based and had a few obvious problems such as poor search engine optimisation, some awkward navigation and text that was too small to read. The result was that our site was hard to find, and if you were lucky enough to find it, it was hard to navigate, and once you navigated where you wanted to go, you couldn't read what was on the page! Just minor stuff! In addition, the portfolio images were very small and didn't stand out or translate well on the rough map texture.

Redesigning the website: solutions developed

Our refreshed hybrid site features a blend of both Flash elements and html coding. One of the goals driving the new site was to capture a broader audience by increasing searchability on the web through the use of html coding for the text and keywords embedded in the text throughout the site. This enables spiders to search beyond the meta tags into secondary and third-level pages. In addition, navigation was pared down to three main categories (ABOUT, WORK, CONTACT) and moved to a fixed point at the top of the home page. No way to miss it now. The overall redesign and layout of the site has been simplified with most of the portfolio

piece featured on a neutral white background, which, in turn, makes the work the hero. The new site also had to continue building on 9Myles' existing brand identity using road-maps and fuel themes while still incorporating our Green sensibilities. The last thing we want is people to think that we're wasting energy using outdated technologies like petrol. Other areas we addressed were highlighted facts displayed in larger text so the viewer could quickly skim through and gain insight into each section without having to read all of the text.

Website launch and results

The new site launched on March 17, 2008 (St. Patrick's Day!), just ahead of our 10th anniversary. Founded in 1998, 9Myles now has a third website since beginning. There are those who think online communications require a technological solution. Online messaging is no more about technology than print advertising is about paper. Online communications is about great ideas. Add easy-to-use interfaces, intuitive navigation and powerful design, and you gain loyal customers and build powerful brands. People say it's a science. It's an art.

Insight

Above all else a website should reflect your company's unique personality. It should be an expression of who you are and what you do. The key is to let the work be the hero and to let your personality shine through. Our process is highly refined brand-positioning, progressive, innovative, and unique. By following a strategic road-map, we build successful brands that make a company's product or service stand out. But real success is achieved by putting our clients in the driver's seat of their industry.

Myles McGuinness is the creative director and principal of **9Myles**, a California-based design studio. Myles holds Bachelor of Arts degrees in both Graphic Design and Photography from Savannah College of Art and Design. With over 10 years of advertising and branding experience, he began his career in North Florida as a designer and art director. He worked for clients such as the NFL's Jacksonville Jaguars, Nissan, and East West Partners. Since moving to San Diego in 1999, Myles has collaborated with some of the area's most recognised industry leaders, including Qualcomm, Red Bull, and the international real estate developer Hines. Myles' designs and photography have been published in Graphis *Logo 6*, *National Geographic*, HOW's *International Design Annual*, Taschen *Logo Design*, *PRINT Magazine Regional Design Annual* and he himself was featured in *Communication Arts*. <**www.9myles.com**>

Neuentwurf des Online-Portfolios
Myles McGuinness

9Myles ist eine kreative Agentur, die auf innovative Weise Menschen mit Marken verbindet. Wir erzeugen Bewusstsein, bauen Kundenbindung auf und lenken Wahrnehmung, indem wir die einzigartigen Ideen entdecken, die Ihr Unternehmen bewegen. 9Myles liefert innovative Lösungen und bahnbrechende Ideen in den Bereichen Brand Development, Corporate Identity, Werbung, Verpackung, Website-Designs, Events und Produktdesign.

Die alte Website und ihre Probleme
Unsere alte Website basierte völlig auf Flash und hatte ein paar kleine, offensichtliche Probleme wie zum Beispiel eine beschämende Suchmaschinenoptimierung, unpraktische Navigation und Text, der zum Lesen zu klein war. Das hatte zur Folge, dass die Site schlecht zu finden war. War man doch dort gelandet, konnte man sich nur schwer darin zurechtfinden. Und wenn man schließlich die Seite gefunden hatte, die einen interessierte, konnte man sie nicht lesen! Wie gesagt – nur kleine Probleme! Darüber hinaus waren die Portfolio-Bilder sehr klein und hoben sich nicht gut von der groben Struktur des Hintergrunds ab.

Die neue Website und ihre Lösungen
Unsere überarbeitete hybride Site mischt Flash-Elemente mit HTML. Eines unserer Ziele war es, durch eine bessere Suchmaschinenoptimierung ein breiteres Publikum zu erreichen. Dies gelang uns durch eine HTML-Codierung des Textes und seiner Schlüsselbegriffe, wodurch Webcrawler über Metatags hinaus auch Seiten auf der zweiten und dritten Siteebene durchsuchen können. Außerdem reduzierten wir die Navigation auf drei Hauptkategorien („Über uns", „Projekte" und „Kontakt") und setzten sie an eine feste Position oben auf der Homepage, wo sie nicht übersehen werden konnten. Das generelle Design der Site wurde vereinfacht: Die meisten Arbeiten aus dem Portfolio stehen nun auf einem neutralen weißen Hintergrund, was ihnen eine stärkere Aussagekraft verleiht. Die neue Site musste auf der bereits bestehenden Identität der Marke 9Myles mit ihren Bildern von Straßenkarten und Tankstellen aufbauen, sollte jedoch auch gleichzeitig ein ökologisches Bewusstsein demonstrieren. Wir wollten auf keinen Fall, dass man von uns denkt, wir würden Energie verschwenden, indem wir altmodische Technologien wie Benzin nutzen. Dann setzten wir noch die Texte größer und hoben die Kernaussagen hervor, sodass der Benutzer schon beim Überfliegen der Seiten einen Eindruck gewinnen kann, ohne gleich den gesamten Text lesen zu müssen.

Launch der Website und Ergebnisse
Die neue Site wurde kurz vor unserem zehnjährigen Jubiläum am 17. März 2008 (St. Patrick's Day!) lanciert. Dies ist die dritte Website seit der Gründung von 9Myles im Jahr 1998. Manche meinen, Online-Kommunikation brauche technische Lösungen. Doch bei Online-Kommunikation geht es genauso wenig um Technik wie bei Printwerbung um Papier. Es geht um großartige Ideen. Fügt man dann noch benutzerfreundliche Oberflächen, eine intuitive Navigation und ein gutes Design hinzu, bekommt man treue Kunden und starke Marken. Das ist keine Wissenschaft, sondern Kunst.

Erkenntnisse
Eine Website sollte in erster Linie die einzigartige Persönlichkeit Ihrer Firma widerspiegeln. Sie sollte Ausdruck dessen sein, wer Sie sind und was Sie machen. Der Schlüssel besteht darin, die Arbeit in den Vorder-

grund zu stellen und dann Ihre Persönlichkeit durch sie hindurch scheinen zu lassen. Unser Prozess ist eine höchst anspruchsvolle Markenpositionierung, die progressiv, innovativ und einzigartig ist. Weil wir einer strategischen Roadmap folgen, bauen wir erfolgreiche Marken auf, durch die die Produkte oder Dienstleistungen einer Firma hervorstechen. Doch die wahren Erfolge fahren wir darüber ein, dass wir unsere Kunden in ihrer Branche ans Steuer setzen.

Myles McGuiness ist der Creative Director und Geschäftsführer von **9Myles**, einer Designagentur in Kalifornien. Myles hat am Savannah College of Art and Design Grafikdesign und Fotografie studiert. Er begann seine Karriere als Designer und Art Director in Florida, wo unter anderem das NFL-Footballteam der Jacksonville Jaguars, Nissan und East West Partners zu seinen Kunden gehörten. Seit er 1999 nach San Diego zog, hat er mit einigen der führenden Wirtschaftsunternehmen der Region zusammengearbeitet, darunter Qualcomm, Red Bull und die internationale Baufirma Hines. Seine Entwürfe und Fotos sind in folgenden Publikationen erschienen: *Logo 6* (Graphis), *National Geographic*, *International Design Annual* (HOW), *Logo Design* (Taschen), *PRINT Magazine Regional Design Annual*. Über Myles McGuinnes erschien ein Artikel in *Communication Arts*. <www.9myles.com>

La reconception des portfolios
Myles McGuinness

9Myles est une société créative de stratégie de marque qui propose une communication innovante pour créer une relation entre le public et les marques. Nous développons la notoriété des marques, fidélisons les clients et influençons la perception en découvrant des idées originales qui accélèrent votre activité. 9Myles imagine des solutions créatives et des idées efficaces dans les domaines du développement de marque, de l'identité d'entreprise, de la publicité, de l'emballage, de la conception de site web, de l'événementiel et de la conception de produit.

L'ancien site web : les problèmes à résoudre
Notre ancien site web était entièrement en Flash et avait quelques problèmes évidents, notamment un mauvais référencement dans les moteurs de recherche, une navigation malaisée et des textes illisibles à cause de la taille des lettres. Résultat : notre site était dur à trouver, et si l'on avait la chance de le trouver, on avait du mal à y naviguer. Et si l'on arrivait à trouver la page que l'on voulait, on ne pouvait pas la lire ! Menues broutilles ! En plus, les images du portfolio étaient très petites et ne se détachaient pas correctement sur le fond à motif de carte.

La reconception du site web : les solutions développées
Notre nouveau site hybride est un mélange d'éléments en Flash et de code HTML. L'un des objectifs était d'attirer un public plus large en améliorant nos résultats dans les moteurs de recherche grâce aux textes et mots-clés que le codage HTML nous a permis de disséminer dans tout le site. Cela permet aux robots d'indexation de chercher au-delà des métas tags, dans les pages de deuxième et troisième niveau.

Nous avons de plus réduit la navigation à trois catégories principales (À PROPOS, TRAVAIL, CONTACT), et nous l'avons cantonnée à un emplacement fixe en haut de la page d'accueil. Maintenant, on ne peut plus la rater. Le site et sa mise en page ont été simplifiés. La plus grande partie du portfolio est présentée sur un fond blanc neutre qui laisse la vedette à notre travail. Le nouveau site devait également continuer dans la lignée de l'identité de marque existante de 9Myles en utilisant des thèmes centrés sur les cartes routières et l'essence, tout en y incorporant notre sensibilité verte. Nous ne voulions surtout pas que les gens pensent que nous gaspillons de l'énergie avec des technologies obsolètes comme le pétrole. Nous avons aussi ajouté des informations rapides à lire en lettres plus grandes pour que les visiteurs puissent parcourir les pages et en saisir le contenu sans avoir besoin de lire tout le texte.

Lancement du site web et résultats
Le nouveau site a été lancé le 17 mars 2008 (le jour de la Saint Patrick !), juste avant notre dixième anniversaire. C'est le troisième site web de 9Myles depuis sa création en 1998. Certains pensent que la communication sur Internet requiert une solution technologique, mais faire passer des messages en ligne n'a pas plus à voir avec la technologie que la publicité dans la presse avec le papier. La communication sur Internet, c'est avant tout la qualité des idées. Ajoutez à cela des interfaces conviviales, une navigation intuitive et un graphisme convaincant, et vous gagnerez des clients fidèles et une marque solide. Certains disent que c'est une science. En fait, c'est un art.

Conseil

Avant tout, un site web doit refléter l'originalité de la personnalité de votre entreprise. Il doit exprimer ce que vous êtes et ce que vous faites. La clé, c'est de donner la vedette au travail et de laisser transparaître votre personnalité. Nous faisons du positionnement de marque très pointu, progressif, innovant et original. En suivant un parcours stratégique, nous bâtissons des marques efficaces qui distinguent le produit ou le service du client par rapport à ses concurrents. Mais le vrai succès, nous l'atteignons en plaçant nos clients aux commandes de leur secteur d'activité.

Myles McGuinness est le directeur de la création et le président de 9Myles, un studio de graphisme californien. Il est titulaire d'une licence en graphisme et en photographie du Savannah College of Art and Design. Il a commencé sa carrière dans le nord de la Floride en tant que graphiste et directeur artistique, et a plus de dix ans d'expérience dans la publicité et la stratégie de marque à son actif. Il a travaillé pour des clients tels que les Jacksonville Jaguars de la NFL, Nissan et East West Partners. Depuis qu'il a déménagé à San Diego en 1999, il a travaillé avec les plus grands noms de la région, notamment Qualcomm, Red Bull et le promoteur immobilier international Hines. Ses œuvres graphiques et photographiques ont été publiées dans *Logo 6* de Graphis, *National Geographic*, la publication *International Design Annual* de HOW, *Logo Design* de Taschen, *PRINT Magazine Regional Design Annual*, et il a lui-même fait l'objet d'un article dans *Communication Arts*.

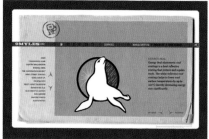

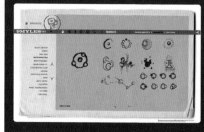

ABOUT
WORK
CONTACT

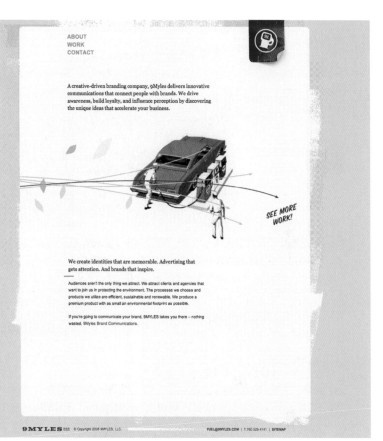

A creative-driven branding company, 9Myles delivers innovative communications that connect people with brands. We drive awareness, build loyalty, and influence perception by discovering the unique ideas that accelerate your business.

SEE MORE WORK!

We create identities that are memorable. Advertising that gets attention. And brands that inspire.

Audiences aren't the only thing we attract. We attract clients and agencies that want to join us in protecting the environment. The processes we choose and products we utilize are efficient, sustainable and renewable. We produce a premium product with as small an environmental footprint as possible.

If you're going to communicate your brand, 9MYLES takes you there – nothing wasted. 9Myles Brand Communications.

9MYLES LLC. © Copyright 2008 9MYLES, LLC.   FUEL@9MYLES.COM | T.760.529.4141 | SITEMAP

Portfolios for Start-ups
James Stone

I'm writing this on a flight back from New York, I don't travel well, so tend to read or doodle, so I'm thankful I've got something to do. I started mimeArtist just six months ago, but have spent ten years writing the name, sketching the logo, and paying the domain name fees. Between my previous job and my new venture I had no time off, but on my first day I had an online presence I was happy for clients and peers to see, and despite the ten-year hiatus, it came together in a weekend...

The key to designing clients' sites is ensuring they fit with the company and their day-to-day operations. I've often met with clients whose sites are neglected for weeks, months, years even, because they require someone full-time to keep it updated, or because it doesn't fit with how the company runs and may create extra work. The majority of my clients are small to medium enterprises who simply can't afford to pay someone to maintain their site, or have key members of staff having to shift focus to the company site where often the site is not the company's main focus; I think the term was "change management" in the first dot-com boom. The same applies to mimeArtist, it is a small business, very small... it's, er... just me!

I needed a site that required minimum effort so I could concentrate on client work. I had to set some hard and fast rules...

First rule, any work on the site should be live. Agencies that show screenshots of a website at the wrong size with no link, even going as far as creating an animation outside of the original brief to portray the site, just to pad out their offering, annoy me. If it is a site and it is online, then the best and most honest way is to link to the site, letting visitors make their own minds up. I don't believe good user experiences

are created through translating Photoshop documents, in the same way as that applies to portfolio sites. I chose to show just enough to identify a project so that the user knows what is being clicked on, and no more. Another reason for this rule is maintenance: making stand-alone versions of sites is time-consuming, and not forward-thinking.

Forward thinking was my second rule. Even if something is online, but not something I want to work on again in the future, I won't show it. I've designed TV ads and DVD interfaces in the past, but being a small company I need to be highly focused; my speciality is interface design, and I don't want noise on my site that detracts from that. Having your own company should be empowering, and you have the potential to choose in some way your own destiny.

Third rule, no Flash... which might sound odd, when almost all my interface work is in Flash. As noted, I look to build systems, engines if you will, that slot into a company and require little input from myself upon launch. On average I get an email less than once a month with a query, purely because I've built a client a system that works with its existing workforce. A good example is a site for a post-production house, which has full-time PR staff, and a machine room that can take grabs of their ads. I created a CMS that split the tasks, and by adding some simple tools like a colour picker skills are pooled, so they have a contemporary and clearly well-considered site. I don't need the same type of system, as I'm not creating new sites every day and so don't need an engine to manage my output, whilst if I want a new feature I can just create it or plug it in. Of course this could be achieved in Flash, but would take longer, and I'd start to input different interaction techniques, when it is just my client work that I want

to sell my services, rather than working to my own unrealistic brief.

Is it working? My current projects have been won because the client has liked something I've done before, or seen the graphic design agencies I've teamed up with. As I complete each project I'm learning what I enjoy doing most and am skewing my site accordingly. It is possibly working too well, I might have to start hiring, and in turn build an engine to keep it running!

James Stone has worked for over ten years in new media, having graduated with first-class honours from Ravensbourne. He has won numerous awards, including a yellow pencil for his work on Compaq Bird while at Edwards Churcher working with Studio AKA, and a BAFTA interactive award for an online version of the film *Bodysong* while at The Mill. In the past few years James was a partner at Engage before going it alone in 2007 to set up **mimeArtist**, where he is currently working on new sites for Studio AKA, SurfaceView, Lucky Voice, and Escape Studios, amongst others. <www.mimeartist.com>

Portfolios für Start-ups
James Stone

Ich schreibe dies, während ich im Flieger zurück von
New York sitze. Da ich ungern fliege, lese oder kritzele
ich meistens und bin also froh, mich damit beschäftigen
zu können. MimeArtist habe ich erst vor sechs Monaten
ins Leben gerufen, verbringe aber schon zehn Jahre
damit, den Namen zu schreiben, das Logo zu skizzieren
und die Gebühren für den Domainnamen zu bezahlen.
Der Wechsel von meinem vorherigen Job zu meiner
neuen Aufgabe erfolgte nahtlos, aber schon am ersten
Tag hatte ich einen Online-Auftritt, den ich Kunden
und Kollegen präsentieren konnte und der – trotz
des zehnjährigen Reifungsprozesses – an nur einem
Wochenende entstand.

Am wichtigsten beim Entwerfen einer Website ist,
dass die Site zum Unternehmen des Kunden passt und
an seinen täglichen Arbeitsabläufen ausgerichtet ist.
Ich habe oft Kunden, deren Sites Wochen, Monate
oder sogar Jahre nicht gepflegt wurden, weil man dafür
jemanden in Vollzeit beschäftigen müsste oder weil
dies nicht in den Arbeitsablauf der Firma passt und
zusätzliche Arbeit macht. Die meisten meiner Kunden
sind kleine bis mittelständische Betriebe, die es sich
nicht leisten können, jemanden zur Pflege der Site
zu engagieren oder einen der Mitarbeiter dafür abzu-
stellen. „Change Management" nannte man das zur
Zeit des ersten Dotcom-Booms. Das Gleiche gilt für
mimeArtist, denn es handelt sich um eine kleine Firma,
eine sehr kleine. Sie besteht nur aus ... mir!

Ich brauchte eine Website mit einem Minimum an
Wartungsaufwand, damit ich mich voll auf die Arbeit
mit den Kunden konzentrieren konnte. Ich musste
also ein paar strenge und knapp gefasste Regeln
aufstellen ...

Regel Nummer eins: Alle Projekte auf der Site sollten
live sein. Mich ärgern Agenturen, die Screenshots
von Websites in falscher Größe und ohne Link abbilden
(manchmal sogar eine gesonderte Animation entwerfen,
die nur dazu dient, die Site anzupreisen). Wenn das
Projekt eine Website ist und diese sich online befindet,
dann ist es am besten und am ehrlichsten, mit der Site
zu verlinken, damit sich die Besucher ihr eigenes Urteil
bilden können. Gute Usererlebnisse entstehen nicht
durch das Umwandeln von Photoshop-Dokumenten, und
das Gleiche gilt auch für Portfolio-Sites. Ich entschied
mich, gerade so viel von einem Projekt zu zeigen, dass
der Besucher weiß, was er anklickt, mehr nicht. Ein
weiterer Grund für diese Regel: Stand-alone-Versionen
von Sites sind zeitaufwendig.

Meine zweite Regel lautet: Nach vorne blicken. Wenn
ein Projekt zwar online ist, aber nicht zu einem Bereich
gehört, mit dem ich mich in Zukunft weiter befassen
möchte, zeige ich es nicht. In der Vergangenheit habe
ich sowohl Fernsehwerbespots als auch DVD-Interfaces
entworfen, doch als kleiner Betrieb muss ich Schwer-
punkte setzen. Meine Spezialität ist Interface-Design,
und deshalb soll es auf meiner Site nichts geben,
was davon ablenkt. Eine eigene Firma zu haben, sollte
bedeuten, dass man die Macht hat, die Richtung zu
bestimmen.

Regel Nummer drei: Kein Flash ... was vielleicht
seltsam klingt, da fast meine gesamte Interface-Arbeit
in Flash erstellt wurde. Wie schon gesagt, möchte ich
Systeme, also sozusagen Arbeitsumgebungen installieren, die sich passgenau in ein Unternehmen einfügen
und nach dem Start von meiner Seite wenig Input
benötigen. Ich bekomme von Kunden im Schnitt weniger
als eine E-Mail-Anfrage pro Monat, weil ich die Site so
angelegt habe, dass der Kunde sie mit den vorhandenen
Arbeitskräften selbst pflegen kann. Ein gutes Beispiel
ist eine Website für eine Post-Production-Firma mit

Vollzeit-PR-Beratern und der Technik, um Standbilder von ihren Werbespots machen zu können. Ich entwickelte ein CMS, mit dem man Aufgaben aufteilen kann, und fügte noch einige einfache Tools wie einen Farbwähler hinzu, sodass die Fähigkeiten der Mitarbeiter kanalisiert wurden. So entstand eine zeitgemäße und gut durchdachte Site. Ich brauche bei mir nicht dasselbe System zu installieren, da ich nicht jeden Tag neue Websites entwerfe und keine eigene Arbeitsumgebung benötige, um meinen Output zu verwalten. Wenn ich die Kundensite durch ein neues Feature ergänzen will, kann ich dieses erstellen und dann einfach in die Arbeitsumgebung des Kunden einpflegen. Das könnte man natürlich auch mit Flash erreichen, aber es würde länger dauern, und ich würde wahrscheinlich anfangen, verschiedene Interaktionstechniken einzubauen und damit über die Bedürfnisse des Kunden hinauszuschießen.

Funktioniert es? Meine laufenden Projekte habe ich bekommen, weil den Kunden etwas an meinen bisherigen Projekten gefiel oder sie die Agenturen mochten, mit denen ich kooperiere. Mit jedem neuen Projekt lerne ich, was ich am liebsten mache, und wandle meine Site entsprechend ab. Vielleicht funktioniert es ja zu gut, und ich muss demnächst Leute anstellen und mir selber eine Arbeitsumgebung bauen, die das Ganze am Laufen hält!

James Stone arbeitet seit über zehn Jahren im Bereich Neue Medien. Er hat sein Studium am Ravensbourne College of Design and Communication mit höchsten Auszeichnungen abgeschlossen und zahlreiche Preise bekommen, darunter während seiner Zeit bei Edwards Churcher einen „Yellow Pencil" für seine Arbeit am Projekt „Compaq Bird" zusammen mit Studio AKA und während seiner Zeit bei The Mill einen BAFTA Interactive Award für eine Online-Version des Films Bodysong. Vor dem Aufbau seiner eigenen Firma war James einige Partner bei Engage. 2007 ging er mit mimeArtist an den Start und arbeitet zurzeit unter anderem an neuen Websites für Studio AKA, Surface View, Lucky Voice und Escape Studios. <www.mimeartist.com>

Les portfolios des start-ups
James Stone

J'écris ceci sur un vol qui me ramène à New York. Je n'aime pas trop voyager, alors j'ai tendance à lire ou à griffonner. Je suis donc bien content d'avoir quelque chose à faire. J'ai créé mimeArtist il a à peine six mois, mais cela fait déjà dix ans que j'écris le nom, que je dessine le logo et que je paie les frais du nom de domaine. Je n'ai pas eu de temps mort entre mon ancien travail et ma nouvelle entreprise, mais dès le premier jour j'avais un site Internet que j'étais content de montrer à mes clients et à mes pairs et, bien que cela ait pris dix ans, tout a été prêt en un week-end...

Dans la conception de sites web, la clé est de s'assurer qu'ils correspondent au client et à ses activités quotidiennes. J'ai souvent rencontré des clients dont les sites sont négligés pendant des semaines, des mois, voire des années, parce qu'ils requièrent une personne à plein temps pour les actualiser, ou parce qu'ils ne s'adaptent pas au mode de fonctionnement de la société et créent du travail supplémentaire. La majorité de mes clients sont de petites ou moyennes entreprises qui ne peuvent tout simplement pas se permettre de payer quelqu'un pour la maintenance de leur site, ni d'obliger des collaborateurs à perdre du temps sur le site alors que souvent ce n'est pas la préoccupation principale de l'entreprise. Je crois qu'à l'époque du premier boom de l'Internet, le terme employé était « gestion du changement ». Le même principe s'applique à mimeArtist. C'est une petite entreprise... toute petite... il n'y a que moi !

Il me fallait un site qui ne me demanderait qu'un minimum d'efforts, pour que je puisse me concentrer sur mes clients. Je me suis fixé des règles très strictes...

Première règle : tous les projets présentés sur le site doivent être des projets actuellement en vigueur.

Cela m'irrite quand je vois des agences qui montrent des captures d'écran d'un site web sans proposer de lien, et qui vont jusqu'à créer une animation qui ne faisait pas partie du projet pour présenter le site, juste pour gonfler leur portfolio. Si le projet est un site et qu'on peut le voir sur Internet, la meilleure manière de procéder, et la plus honnête, est de proposer un lien et de laisser les visiteurs se faire leur propre opinion. Je ne pense pas que l'on crée une expérience agréable pour les utilisateurs en traduisant des documents Photoshop, et cela s'applique également aux sites de portfolio. J'ai décidé de ne montrer que le minimum pour identifier les projets afin que le visiteur sache ce sur quoi il clique, mais pas plus. Le facteur de la maintenance plaide aussi en faveur de cette règle : la création de versions autonomes des sites prend beaucoup de temps, et ce n'est pas une démarche très proactive.

La proactivité est ma deuxième règle. Si l'un de mes projets est actuellement en ligne, mais que je ne souhaite pas refaire le même genre de chose à l'avenir, je ne le présente pas dans mon portfolio. J'ai déjà conçu des spots TV et des interfaces de DVD, mais comme je suis une petite entreprise je dois me concentrer sur une seule activité. Ma spécialité, c'est la conception d'interfaces, et je ne veux pas que mon site contienne des éléments qui puissent suggérer le contraire. Le fait d'avoir sa propre entreprise devrait donner les moyens de choisir son propre chemin.

Troisième règle : pas de Flash... Ce qui pourrait sembler étrange, puisque presque toutes mes interfaces sont en Flash. Comme je l'ai déjà dit, j'essaie de bâtir des systèmes, des moteurs, si l'on veut, qui trouvent leur place au sein d'une entreprise et qui me demandent peu d'efforts après leur mise en place. En

www.mimeartist.com

moyenne, je reçois moins d'une question par mois, tout simplement parce que j'ai créé un système qui fonctionne avec la structure existante de l'entreprise. Je prendrai comme exemple un site que j'ai conçu pour une maison de postproduction qui a une équipe de relations publiques et les équipements nécessaires pour prendre des échantillons de leurs publicités. J'ai créé un système de gestion des contenus qui divise les tâches, et en y ajoutant quelques outils simples, comme un sélectionneur de couleurs, les compétences sont canalisées, ce qui donne à ce client un site contemporain et respecté. Je n'ai pas besoin du même type de système, parce que je ne crée pas des nouveaux sites chaque jour et je n'ai donc pas besoin d'un moteur pour gérer mes projets, et si je veux une nouvelle fonction je n'ai qu'à la créer ou la rattacher au reste. Bien sûr, je pourrais faire la même chose en Flash, mais cela prendrait plus de temps, et je commencerais à avoir besoin de différentes techniques d'interaction. Alors que ce que je veux, c'est que mes projets fassent la publicité de mes services, et non passer du temps sur un site irréaliste.

Cela fonctionne-t-il ? Mes projets actuels m'ont été attribués parce que le client a aimé l'un de mes projets précédents, ou a vu l'une des agences de graphisme avec lesquelles j'ai fait équipe. Chaque fois que je termine un projet, j'en apprends davantage sur ce que j'aime faire le plus, et j'oriente mon site en conséquence. Cela fonctionne même peut-être trop bien, il va falloir que j'embauche, et que je crée un moteur pour faire tourner le site !

James Stone a travaillé pendant plus de dix ans dans les nouveaux médias, et est diplômé avec mention de Ravensbourne. Il a remporté de nombreuses récompenses, notamment un prix Yellow Pencil pour son travail sur « Compaq Bird » lorsqu'il était chez Edwards Churcher en collaboration avec Studio AKA, et un prix BAFTA Interactive pour une version Internet du film *Bodysong* lorsqu'il était chez The Mill. Ces dernières années, il a été associé chez Engage avant de se lancer en indépendant et de créer mimeArtist en 2007. Il y travaille actuellement sur de nouveaux sites pour Studio AKA, SurfaceView, Lucky Voice et Escape Studios, entre autres.

Interview
Postgal Workshop

How important is an online portfolio for you?

It is very important for us because it allows us to showcase work online in real time. Works such as doll-doll.com, which is a blogpet, can be demonstrated on the fly and their effect on users' blogs, if users can be measured directly. Prospective clients can always see the effectiveness by counting how many real blogs have installed this blogpet, for instance, one of the best ways to prove that the project really works!

How many people access your portfolio online?

Around 70,000 people per month.

How do you pitch to clients in HK using online portfolios?

We frequently send our portfolio in CD and other electronic formats. Our website has a "feedback" section where new clients can also contact us directly.

Does the online portfolio help you to get work from other regions?

Yes, definitely. It's a great platform for showing our talents and advantages.

How often do you upload new works on to the website?

Around once or twice a month.

How do you see the creative industry in Hong Kong?

We see today two clear changes in the market. The good side is that in recent years we have seen that many Hong Kong / Chinese designers have become much more well received internationally. We think it's a really good trend for people to see Hong Kong's creative side growing. On the other hand, commercially speaking,

we are aware that some designers offer really competitive deals, but with poor quality of output. The regional market is such that not everyone accords the same value for a good design, and critical reception of work varies a lot. If the basic requirement for being a designer is only to know how to operate Adobe Photoshop, as many might think, then many people would be entitled to work as a designer.

How have you been building up your portfolio?

For us, there is a basic simple vision: in most cases, good design does not require a very powerful effect, and using a simple way to present a concept is good enough, like a cursor, that becomes a tree, where you can grow more trees by clicking again and again across the screen. Creative ideas are slightly ridiculous sometimes, and these are interesting and innovative concepts that other people haven't yet considered. There is no way you can rely on technology alone.

What you can expect for the future...

We hope to be able to create more new things, and lead the way, by working with new technologies as they emerge. With increasing internet speed one can play a video on YouTube within 10 seconds of logging on to the site, so animation and video can be easily combined with interactive features. More and more, interesting programming effects will also allow the creation of new media, which will offer better interactive capabilities between users and promote deeper engagement.

www.postgal.com

Postgal Workshop is a multimedia and animation creative team based in Hong Kong, working with clients such as Coca-Cola, Nike, Nokia, DHL, Levi's, Hong Kong Asian Film Festival and East Asian Games. Postgal has been invited to the Milia Digital conference in Cannes, France, Kinolab in Poland, HK TVB (TV) in Hong Kong, FM 903 Radio, and the Hong Kong Baptist University, to share views on design and communication. Postgal is also on the jury for the Coca-Cola Art Bottle Competition. <**www.postgal.com**>

Interview
Postgal Workshop

Wie wichtig ist ein Online-Portfolio für euch?
Sehr wichtig, weil wir damit in Echtzeit unsere Arbeit online präsentieren können. Projekte wie das Blogpet doll-doll.com können jederzeit spontan aufgerufen werden, und ihre Wirkung auf die Blogs der User lässt sich direkt abmessen. Potenzielle Kunden können den Erfolg überprüfen, indem sie abzählen, wie viele echte Blogs das Blogpet installiert haben – eine hervorragende Methode, um zu beweisen, dass das Projekt tatsächlich funktioniert!

Wie viele Menschen greifen auf euer Online-Portfolio zu?
Etwa 70.000 im Monat.

Wie präsentiert ihr euch anhand des Online-Portfolios vor Kunden in Hongkong?
Wir verschicken die Portfolios oft als CD oder in anderen elektronischen Formaten. Unsere Website hat eine „Feedback"-Funktion, mit der neue Kunden uns direkt kontaktieren können.

Hilft euch das Online-Portfolio dabei, Aufträge aus anderen Ländern zu bekommen?
Ja, auf jeden Fall. Es ist eine großartige Plattform, um unsere Fähigkeiten und Vorzüge zu präsentieren.

Wie oft ladet ihr neue Projekte auf die Website hoch?
Ungefähr ein- oder zweimal im Monat.

Wie schätzt ihr den Markt für Grafikdesign in Hongkong ein?
Wir sehen ganz deutlich zwei Veränderungen: Die gute ist, dass in den letzten Jahren viele Künstler aus Hongkong bzw. China internationale Anerkennung

erfahren haben. Leute sehen, wie die kreative Seite in Hongkong wächst. Auf der anderen Seite sind wir uns bewusst, dass manche Designer zwar sehr preiswert sind, aber schlechte Qualität liefern. Auf dem regionalen Markt legt nicht jeder Wert auf gutes Design, und die Bewertung der Qualität schwankt sehr. Wenn das einzige Kriterium für den Beruf des Grafikdesigners die Beherrschung von Adobe Photoshop wäre, wie viele denken, dann könnten sehr viele Menschen als Designer arbeiten.

Wie ist euer Portfolio aufgebaut?
Unsere grundlegende Vision ist einfach. Meistens braucht gutes Design keine aufwendigen Effekte. Es reicht aus, ein Konzept auf einfache Art zu präsentieren, wie ein Cursor, der zu einem Baum wird und mit dem man durch Klicken auf den Bildschirm weitere Bäume pflanzen kann. Kreative Ideen wirken manchmal etwas lächerlich. Das sind dann oft interessante und innovative Konzepte, auf die vorher noch niemand gekommen ist. Man kann sich nicht nur auf die Technik verlassen.

Was wird die Zukunft bringen?
Wir möchten viele neue Projekte realisieren und bei der Verwendung neuer Technologien Vorreiter sein. Mit zunehmender Internetgeschwindigkeit kann man ein Video auf YouTube innerhalb von 10 Sekunden nach Einloggen auf die Site abspielen. Animation und Video lassen sich also leicht mit interaktiven Elementen kombinieren. Interessante Programmiereffekte werden verstärkt neue Medien hervorbringen, die die Interaktionsmöglichkeiten zwischen Usern verbessern und ein stärkeres persönliches Engagement ermöglichen.

www.postgal.com

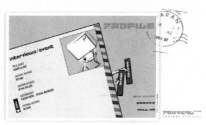

Postgal Workshop ist ein in Hongkong ansässiges Designteam
für Multimedia und Animation und zählt unter anderem Coca-Cola,
Nike, Nokia, DHL, Levi's, das Hongkong Asian Film Festival und die
East Asian Games zu seinen Kunden. Postgal wurde zu vielen
Veranstaltungen und Institutionen eingeladen, um über Design
und Kommunikation zu referieren, z.B. Milia Digital Conference in
Cannes, Kinolab in Polen, HK TVB (TV) in Hongkong, FM 903 Radio
und die Hong Kong Baptist University. Postgal ist auch
Jurymitglied bei der Coca-Cola Art Bottle Competition.

Entretien
Postgal Workshop

Est-ce important pour vous d'avoir un portfolio sur Internet ?

C'est très important, car cela nous permet de présenter notre travail en temps réel. On peut présenter sur-le-champ des projets comme doll-doll.com, qui est un site de blogpets (compagnons de blog), et leur effet sur le blog des utilisateurs est mesurable en direct. Par exemple, les clients potentiels peuvent toujours constater l'efficacité en comptant le nombre de blogs réels qui ont installé ce blogpet, c'est l'une des meilleures façons de prouver que le projet fonctionne vraiment !

Combien de personnes voient votre portfolio sur Internet ?

Environ 70 000 personnes par mois.

Comment vous présentez-vous à vos clients de Hong Kong avec vos portfolios en ligne ?

Nous envoyons souvent notre portfolio sur CD, ou sous d'autres formats électroniques. Notre site web a une partie « feedback » qui permet aux nouveaux clients de nous contacter directement.

Le portfolio de votre site vous aide-t-il à trouver du travail dans d'autres régions du monde ?

Oui, sans aucun doute. C'est une excellente plateforme pour présenter nos talents et nos avantages.

À quelle fréquence ajoutez-vous de nouveaux projets à votre site web ?

Environ une ou deux fois par mois.

Que pensez-vous du secteur de la créativité à Hong Kong ?

Actuellement, nous voyons deux changements très

clairs sur le marché. Le bon côté, c'est que ces dernières années nous avons vu que beaucoup de concepteurs de Hong Kong ou de Chine sont beaucoup mieux reçus sur la scène internationale. C'est une très bonne chose que les gens voient que le secteur de la créativité est en pleine croissance à Hong Kong. D'un autre côté, d'un point de vue commercial, nous savons que certains concepteurs proposent de travailler à un prix très concurrentiel, mais avec des résultats médiocres. La configuration du marché régional fait que tout le monde n'accorde pas la même valeur à la qualité de la réalisation, et l'accueil critique est très variable. Si pour être concepteur il suffit de savoir se servir d'Adobe Photoshop, comme beaucoup le croient, alors beaucoup de gens peuvent se considérer qualifiés pour travailler dans ce domaine.

Comment avez-vous construit votre portfolio ?

Pour nous, il y a une vision de départ très simple : dans la plupart des cas, les bons projets n'ont pas besoin d'effets bluffants, et il suffit de les présenter en toute simplicité. Par exemple avec un curseur qui devient un arbre, où l'on peut faire pousser d'autres arbres en cliquant sur l'écran. Parfois les idées créatives sont un peu ridicules, car ce sont des concepts intéressants et innovants que personne d'autre n'avait encore imaginés. On ne peut pas se reposer entièrement sur la technologie.

Que vous réserve l'avenir...

Nous espérons pouvoir continuer à créer des nouveautés, et à montrer le chemin en travaillant sur les nouvelles technologies. Avec la croissance de la vitesse de connexion, on peut voir une vidéo sur YouTube dans les 10 secondes qui suivent l'arrivée sur le site, alors

ont peut facilement combiner l'animation et la vidéo à des fonctions interactives. De plus en plus, des effets de programmation intéressants permettront de créer de nouveaux supports, qui offriront de meilleures options d'interactivité entre les utilisateurs et favoriseront une expérience plus engageante.

Postgal Workshop est une équipe créative qui travaille à Hong Kong dans les domaines du multimédia et de l'interactivité, et qui a pour clients Coca-Cola, Nike, Nokia, DHL, Levi's, Hong Kong Asian Film Festival et East Asian Games, entre autres. L'équipe de Postgal a été invitée à la conférence Milia Digital à Cannes, en France, à Kinolab en Pologne, sur HK TVB (TV) à Hong Kong, sur FM 903 Radio, et à l'Université Baptiste de Hong Kong pour partager ses vues sur le design et la communication. Postgal fait également partie du jury pour le concours Coca-Cola Art Bottle. <**www.postgal.com**>

Info

DESIGN STUDIO: Vergani & Gasco <www.technemedia.it>. /// **DESIGN:** Luigi Vergani, Nicola Gasco. /// **PROGRAMMING:** Luigi Vergani, Nicola Gasco. /// **CONTENTS:** Photo, text. /// **TYPE:** Bathroom Furniture Design. /// **CLIENT:** 2B Italia S.r.l. /// **TOOLS:** Flash, PHP, XML, MySQL, Photoshop, Illustrator. /// **AWARDS:** FWA (Site of the Day), Design Licks, The Best Designs.com, DesignCharts, NewWebPick, Netdiver, gouw.nu, Linkage, Spyline, Flash Mania. /// **COST:** 4 weeks.

DESIGN STUDIO: Huncwot <www.huncwot.com>. /// **DESIGN:** Arek Romanski, Lukasz Knasiecki. /// **PROGRAMMING:** Arek Romanski, Lukasz Knasiecki. /// **CONTENTS:** Video, photo, music, text. /// **TYPE:** Theather group. /// **CLIENT:** 2xU Usta Usta Theather. /// **TOOLS:** Photoshop, Final Cut, Freehand, Flash, PHP/SQL. /// **AWARDS:** Digital Thread. /// **COST:** 200 hours.

Info

DESIGN STUDIO: Simone Inc. <www.ilovesimone.com>. /// DESIGN: Kaie Murakami (Art Direction); Rintaro Iwashita (Design). /// PROGRAMMING:
Akihiko Ono. /// CONTENTS: Music, video, text. /// TYPE: Record label. /// CLIENT: Acehigh Records. /// TOOLS: Flash, XML, FLV, Photoshop. ///
AWARDS: e-Creative (Site of the Day). /// COST: 120 hours.

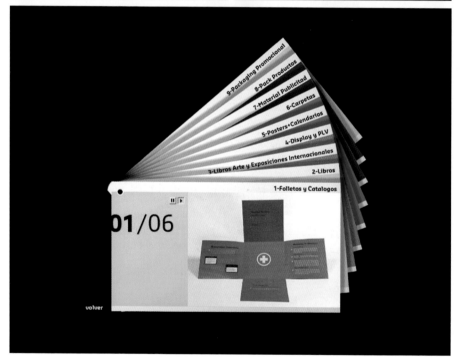

Info

DESIGN STUDIO: elespacio <www.elespacio.net>. /// **DESIGN:** Juanmi Sansinenea, Agnieszka Sekreta. /// **PROGRAMMING:** Juanmi Sansinenea; Alt120 <alt120.com>. /// **CONTENTS:** Photo, text. /// **TYPE:** Printer. /// **CLIENT:** Alfadir. /// **TOOLS:** Photoshop, Flash. /// **COST:** 3 months.

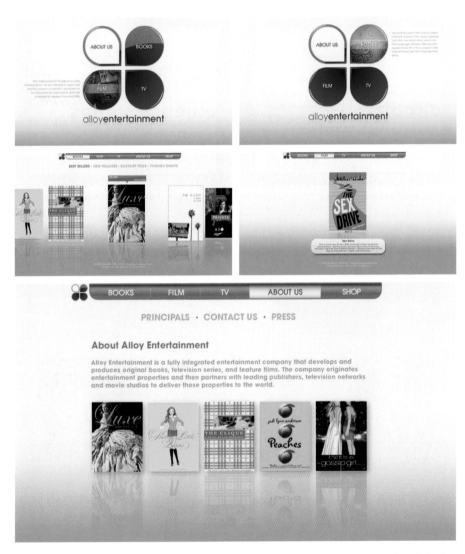

Info

DESIGN STUDIO: Liquid Color Media <www.liquidcolormedia.com>; multimediaHAAM <www.multimediahaam.com>. /// **DESIGN:** Davey Woodward, Jack Manno, Aragorn Ligocki. /// **PROGRAMMING:** Aragorn Ligocki. /// **CONTENTS:** Photo, text. /// **TYPE:** Publishing. /// **CLIENT:** Alloy Entertainment. /// **TOOLS:** Flash, ActionScript, Photoshop, Illustrator.

Info

DESIGN STUDIO: Andy Foulds Design <www.andyfoulds.co.uk>. /// DESIGN: Andy Foulds. /// PROGRAMMING: Andy Foulds. CONTENTS: Photo, text. ///
TYPE: Freelance designer. /// TOOLS: Flash, HTML, XML, Homesite, Photoshop. /// AWARDS: Flashforward, FWA, FlashKit.

Info

DESIGN STUDIO: Simone Inc. <www.ilovesimone.com>. /// DESIGN: Kaie Murakami, Sin Masuda (Art Direction); Hiroyuki Misono (Design). /// PROGRAMMING: Hiroyuki Misono (Interactive Designer). /// CONTENTS: Photo, text. /// TYPE: Artists' management office. /// CLIENT: Angle Management Produce. /// TOOLS: Flash, XML. /// COST: 50 hours.

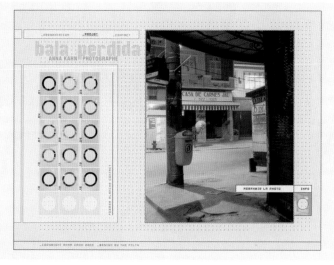

Info

DESIGN STUDIO: The Filth <www.the-filth.com>. /// **PROGRAMMING:** Lucile Dunyack. /// **CONTENTS:** Photo, text. /// **TYPE:** Photographer. ///
CLIENT: Anna Kanh. /// **TOOLS:** Flash.

DESIGN STUDIO: Hello Monday <www.hellomonday.com>. /// **DESIGN:** Hello Monday. /// **PROGRAMMING:** Hello Monday. /// **CONTENTS:** Photo, text. ///
TYPE: Design studio. /// **CLIENT:** Minus. /// **TOOLS:** Flash, Flex, XML, PHP, Photoshop, After Effects. /// **AWARDS:** NewWebPick, Webby Awards,
DesignCharts. /// **COST:** 145 hours.

Info

DESIGN STUDIO: Danka Studio <www.dankastudio.fr>. /// **DESIGN:** Guillaume Bonnecase. /// **PROGRAMMING:** Grégoire Gerardin. /// **CONTENTS:** Photo, text. /// **TYPE:** Digital imagery studio. /// **CLIENT:** Asylum. /// **TOOLS:** Photoshop, Flash, XML, PHP. /// **AWARDS:** FWA (Site of the Day). /// **COST:** 150–200 hours.

AXE SAÔNE

www.axesaone.fr

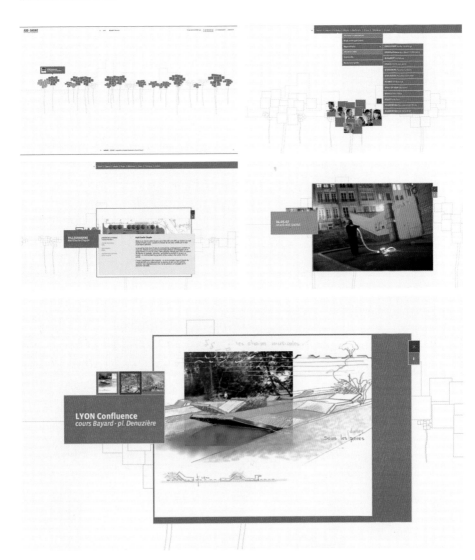

Info

DESIGN STUDIO: Danka Studio <www.dankastudio.fr>. /// DESIGN: Guillaume Bonnecase. /// PROGRAMMING: Grégoire Gérardin. /// CONTENTS: Photo, text. /// TYPE: Architecture studio. /// CLIENT: Axe Saône Architectes Paysagistes. /// TOOLS: Photoshop, Flash, XML, PHP. /// AWARDS: FWA (Site of the Day). /// COST: 150–200 hours.

AZAM

www.azam.com

DESIGN STUDIO: Square Circle Media <www.sqcircle.com>. /// **DESIGN:** Danny Burnside, Adam Pilarski, Stella Jordan. /// **PROGRAMMING:** George Medve, Chris Sees. /// **CONTENTS:** Photo, text. /// **TYPE:** Artist. /// **CLIENT:** Azam Gallery. /// **TOOLS:** Flash, Eclipse, Cinema 4D, Photoshop, PHPeclipse (Eclipse plug-in), After Effects. /// **COST:** £15,000.

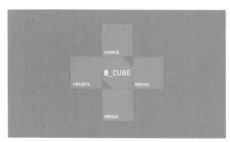

Info

DESIGN STUDIO: Danka Studio <www.dankastudio.fr>. /// DESIGN: Guillaume Bonnecase. /// PROGRAMMING: Grégoire Gerardin. /// CONTENTS: Photo, text. /// TYPE: Architecture studio. /// CLIENT: B_Cube Architectes Associés. /// TOOLS: Photoshop, Flash, XML, PHP. /// AWARDS: FWA (Site of the Day). /// COST: 150–200 hours.

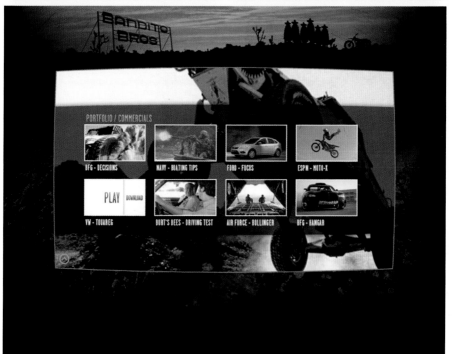

Info

DESIGN STUDIO: Geyrhalter Design <www.geyrhalter.com>. /// DESIGN: Fabian Geyrhalter, Bobby Dragulescu. /// PROGRAMMING: Matt Inauen. ///
CONTENTS: Video, photo, text. /// TYPE: Production studio. /// CLIENT: Bandito Brothers. /// TOOLS: XML, Flash, Photoshop.

Info

DESIGN STUDIO: BASICS09 <www.basics09.de>. /// DESIGN: Arne Fehmel, Korbinian Kainz, Roland Brückner, Rasso Hilber. /// PROGRAMMING: Rasso Hilber. /// CONTENTS: Photo, illustration, text. /// TYPE: Design Studio. /// TOOLS: Photoshop, Flash, XHTML, CSS, Javascript. /// AWARDS: FWA (Site of the Day), DesignCharts, DOPE Awards. /// COST: 4 weeks.

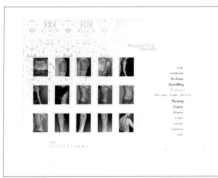

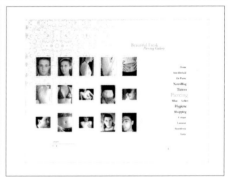

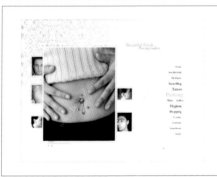

DESIGN STUDIO: Chilli Design & Multimedia <www.chilli.be>. /// **DESIGN:** Frederik Vanderfaeillie. /// **PROGRAMMING:** Gaëtan Lafaut. /// **CONTENTS:** Photo, text. /// **TYPE:** Tattoo artist and illustrator. /// **CLIENT:** Beautiful Freak Studio. /// **TOOLS:** Photoshop, Flash. /// **AWARDS:** DOPE Awards, StandOut Award, Creative Website Awards, Design Licks. /// **COST:** 110 hours.

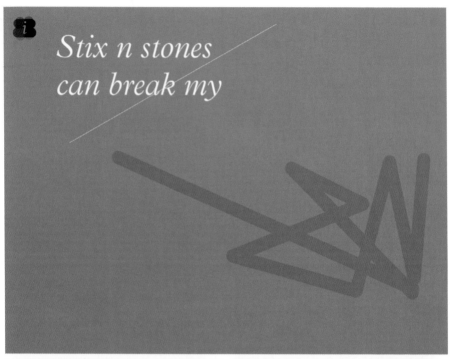

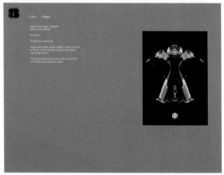

Info · **DESIGN STUDIO:** Beautiful Information <www.beautifulinformation.com>. /// **DESIGN:** Rade Milicevic. /// **PROGRAMMING:** Rade Milicevic. /// **CONTENTS:** Photo, text. /// **TYPE:** Graphic and web designer. /// **TOOLS:** Flash. /// **COST:** 170 hours.

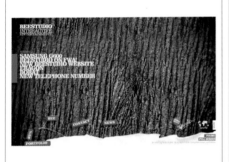

Info

DESIGN STUDIO: Beestudio <www.beestudio.pl>. /// DESIGN: Paweł Schedler (Creative Director); Piotr Korczynski (Motion Design). /// PROGRAMMING: Grzegorz Burnos, Jacek Apanasik. /// CONTENTS: Animation, motion-graphics, video, music, text. /// TYPE: Interactive agency. /// TOOLS: Flash, Photoshop, XML, PHP, MySQL, Combustion, 3d Studio Max. /// AWARDS: FWA (Site of the Day), TAXI (Site of the Day). /// COST: 150 hours.

Info

DESIGN STUDIO: Loyal Design <www.thisisloyal.com>. /// **DESIGN:** Loyal Design. /// **PROGRAMMING:** Loyal Design. /// **CONTENTS:** Music, video, motion-graphics, animation, illustration, photo, text. /// **TYPE:** Designers and art directors. /// **CLIENT:** Bigstar. /// **TOOLS:** Photoshop, Flash, HTML, PHP. /// **COST:** 480 hours.

BLUEMETAL

www.bluemetalcorp.com

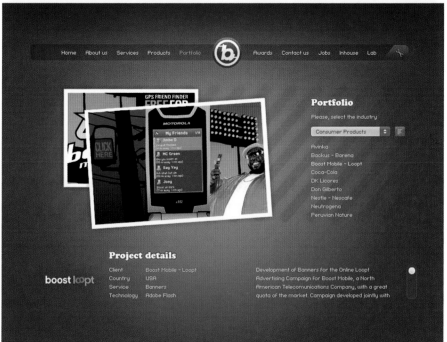

DESIGN STUDIO: Global Interactive Firm <www.bluemetalcorp.com>. /// **DESIGN:** Bluemetal. /// **PROGRAMMING:** Bluemetal. /// **CONTENTS:** Photo, text. /// **TYPE:** Interactive agency. /// **TOOLS:** Flash, Photoshop, Dreamweaver, Custom CMS, PHP, MySQL, Autodesk 3d Studio Max. /// **AWARDS:** Lookom, Plasticpilots, American Website Awards, Art Today, Catalizado, CSS Flash, Design Licks, Latin Website Awards. /// **COST:** 1 month.

DESIGN STUDIO: Openfield Creative <www.openfieldcreative.com>. /// **DESIGN:** Brandon Blangger, Brian Keenan (Creative Direction); Josh Barnes (Strategy Director); Matt Broerman (Design Director). /// **PROGRAMMING:** Matt Broerman. /// **CONTENTS:** Illustration, photo, animation. /// **TYPE:** 3d architectural rendering and animation studio. /// **CLIENT:** Bowen Studios. /// **TOOLS:** Flash, AS2, XML, Photoshop, Illustrator. /// **AWARDS:** FWA (Site of the Day), DOPE Awards. /// **COST:** 110 hours.

bsur.com
an impression of past, present and future projects
best viewed at 1024x768px

bs ur con sul ting

building a strong brand is a matter of finding yourself. define the true essence of your brand. unlock your values. visualize your mentality. then live that essence every day. aim to get all the brand cues right. bsur is a dutch international group of companies, creating and re-engineering brands and brand communication platforms. we are independently operating companies guided by the same solid principle: increasing the value of your brand

> **bsurconsulting**
brand portfolio creativity
brand re-engineering
brand creation

> **bsuragency**
brand identity design
integrated communications
brand activation

> **bsurfactory**
prepress and production
international roll-out
customized ordering systems

www.bsur.com return on branding

© bsur 2008 |

Info

DESIGN STUDIO: BSUR.com <www.bsur.com>. /// **DESIGN:** Robbie Hoesman. /// **PROGRAMMING:** 10mg: Marc Selhorst, Demmy Onink Flash; Poort80 (Database). /// **CONTENTS:** Photo, video, text. /// **TYPE:** Advertising and branding agency. /// **TOOLS:** Flash.

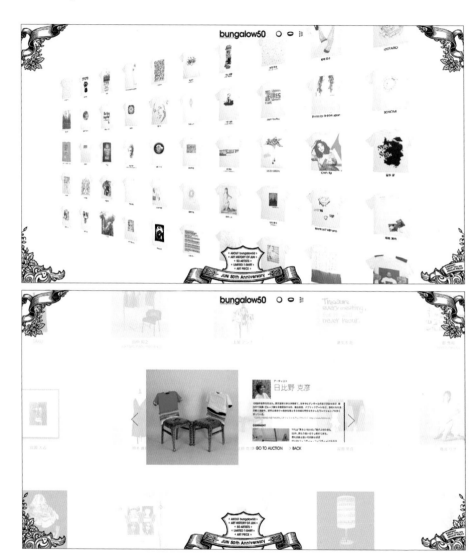

Info

DESIGN STUDIO: Simone Inc. <www.ilovesimone.com>. /// DESIGN: Kaie Murakami (Art Direction); Hiroyuki Misono (Design). /// PROGRAMMING: Hiroyuki Misono (Interactive Designer). /// CONTENTS: Photo, 3d, motion-graphics. /// TYPE: Fashion brand. /// CLIENT: Jun Co., Ltd. /// TOOLS: Flash, XML. /// COST: 100 hours.

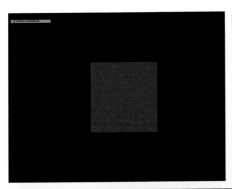

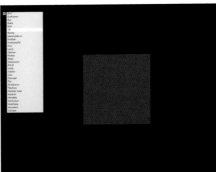

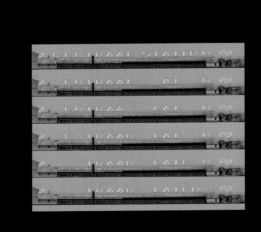

Info

DESIGN STUDIO: DC <www.dcworks.nl>. /// **DESIGN:** Martijn Rietveld, Joey Vermijs, Maarten Mieras. /// **PROGRAMMING:** Maarten Mieras, Merijn van Essen. /// **CONTENTS:** Photo, text. /// **TYPE:** Industrial design and architecture studio. /// **CLIENT:** Bureau Lakenvelder. /// **TOOLS:** Flash, XML. /// **COST:** 100 hours.

CAO GUIMARÃES

www.caoguimaraes.com

BRAZIL

2007

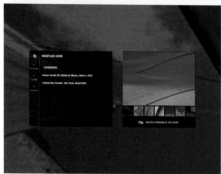

DESIGN STUDIO: Osso <www.osso.com.br>. /// DESIGN: Fred Paulino (Art Director/Conception); João Henrique Wilbert, Paulo Barcelos (Design); Laura Barbi (Project Manager). /// PROGRAMMING: Fred Paulino, João Henrique Wilbert, Paulo Barcelos, Fabricio Ferraz, Julião Villas. /// CONTENTS: Photo, video, text. /// TYPE: Artist, photographer and filmmaker. /// CLIENT: Cao Guimarães. /// TOOLS: Dreamweaver, HTML, XML, Flash, Photoshop. /// COST: 240 hours.

CARLOS ANN / DESCARADO

www.carlosann.com/descarado

SPAIN

2005

Info

DESIGN STUDIO: area3 <www.area3.net>. /// **DESIGN:** Sebastián Puiggrós, Chema Longobardo. /// **PROGRAMMING:** Federico Joselevich. /// **CONTENTS:** Illustration, photo, animation, music. /// **TYPE:** Musician. /// **CLIENT:** Carlos Ann. /// **TOOLS:** Flash. /// **AWARDS:** Barcelona Visual Sound.

CENTRE OF CONTEMPORARY ART POLAND

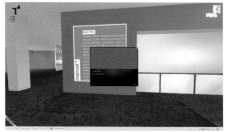

Info

DESIGN STUDIO: Beestudio <www.beestudio.pl>. /// **DESIGN:** Paweł Schedler (Creative Director); Piotr Korczynski (Motion Design). /// **PROGRAMMING:** Grzegorz Burnos, Jacek Apanasik. /// **CONTENTS:** Photo, illustration, animation, motion-graphics, video, music, text. /// **TYPE:** Centre of Contemporary Art. /// **CLIENT:** Centre of Contemporary Art in Torun. /// **TOOLS:** Flash, Photoshop, PV3D, Sketchup, 3d Studio Max, PHP, PostgreSQL, Combustion. /// **AWARDS:** FWA (Site of the Day). /// **COST:** 640 hours.

Info

DESIGN STUDIO: DC <www.dcworks.nl>. /// DESIGN: Joey Vermijs, Matijn Rietveld, Harm van de Ven. /// PROGRAMMING: Harm van de Ven. ///
CONTENTS: Music, video, photo. /// TYPE: Singer, musician. /// CLIENT: Charlie Dee. /// TOOLS: Flash, XML. /// COST: 350 hours.

Info

DESIGN STUDIO: Cheval de Troie <http://blog.chevaldetroie.net>. /// CONTENTS: Photo, text, game. /// TYPE: Agency. /// TOOLS: Flash, Illustrator, Photoshop. /// AWARDS: FWA (Site of the Day), DOPE Awards, DesignCharts, Design Licks.

DESIGN STUDIO: Chilli Design & Multimedia <www.chilli.be>. /// **DESIGN:** Frederik Vanderfaeillie. /// **PROGRAMMING:** Gaëtan Lafaut. /// **CONTENTS:** Photo, text, animation. /// **TYPE:** Design, multimedia, and advertising agency. /// **TOOLS:** Photoshop, Flash, MySQL database. /// **AWARDS:** The Best Designs.com, Lookom, DOPE Awards. /// **COST:** 80 hours.

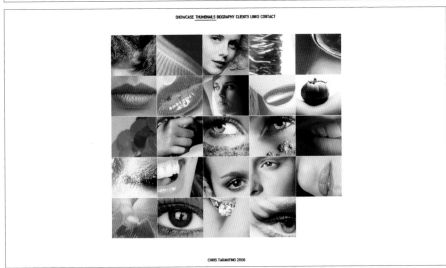

Info

DESIGN STUDIO: HELLOHELLO!! <www.hellohello.bz>. /// **DESIGN:** Thierry Loa "Dr. Hello". /// **PROGRAMMING:** Thierry Loa "Dr. Hello", Clayton Partridge. /// **CONTENTS:** Animation, photo. /// **TYPE:** Photo retoucher. /// **CLIENT:** Chris Tarantino. /// **TOOLS:** Flash, Coldfusion. /// **COST:** 6 weeks.

Info

DESIGN STUDIO: Grand Creative <www.wearegrand.com>. /// **DESIGN:** Luke Canning. /// **PROGRAMMING:** Matthew Quinn. /// **CONTENTS:** Photo. ///
TYPE: Photographer. /// **CLIENT:** Chris Woods. /// **TOOLS:** Photoshop, Illustrator, Flash, Coda, Transmit. /// **AWARDS:** ADCC.

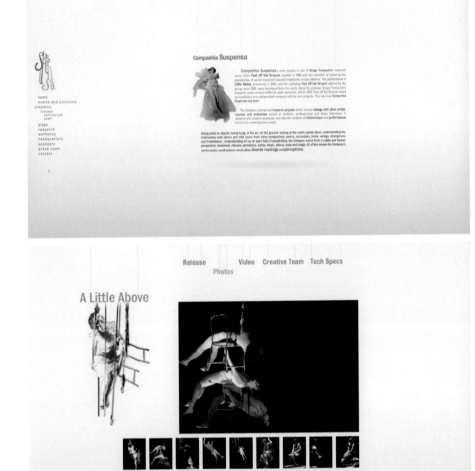

Info

DESIGN STUDIO: Osso <www.osso.com.br>. /// **DESIGN:** Fred Paulino (Art Direction/Conception); Paulo Barcelos, Julião Villas (Design); Laura Barbi (Project Manager). /// **PROGRAMMING:** Fred Paulino, Paulo Barcelos, Julião Villas. /// **CONTENTS:** Photo, text. /// **TYPE:** Performance company. /// **CLIENT:** Companhia Suspensa. /// **TOOLS:** XML, Flash, Photoshop. /// **COST:** 240 hours.

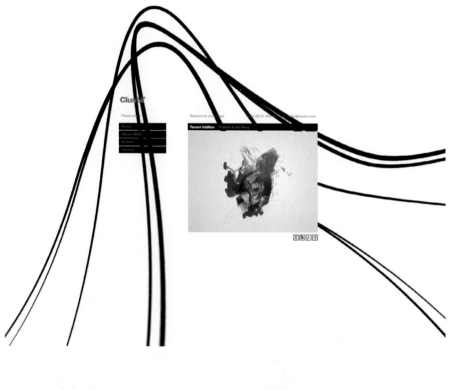

Info

DESIGN STUDIO: Clusta <www.clusta.com>. /// **DESIGN:** Matt Clugston, Arran Aver, Martin Donnelly. /// **PROGRAMMING:** Sean Duffy. /// **CONTENTS:** Illustration, music, animation, motion-graphics, print, film, photo. /// **TYPE:** Design studio. /// **TOOLS:** Flash, ActionScript, XML, ASP.net, Photoshop, After Effects.

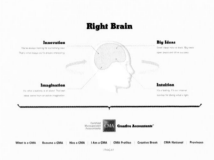

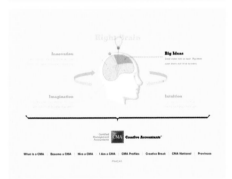

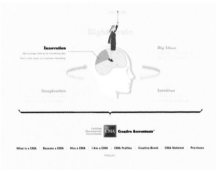

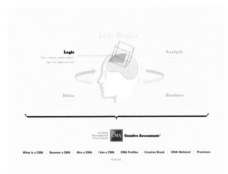

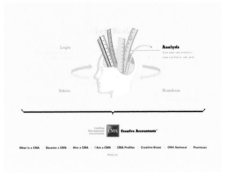

DESIGN STUDIO: Grand Creative <www.wearegrand.com>. /// **DESIGN:** TBWA\Toronto: Noel Fenn; Grand Creative: Luke Canning. /// **PROGRAMMING:** Kavin Wong. /// **CONTENTS:** Animation, text, illustration. /// **TYPE:** Accountants. /// **CLIENT:** TBWA\Toronto (Certified Management Accountants). /// **TOOLS:** Photoshop, Illustrator, Flash, Coda, Transmit.

Info

DESIGN STUDIO: Cookie <www.cookie.pl>. /// DESIGN: Lukasz Twardowski, Mariusz Kucharczyk. /// PROGRAMMING: Lukasz Twardowski, Marcin Warpechowski. /// CONTENTS: Illustration, photo, animation. /// TYPE: Design, interactive and creative agency. /// CLIENT: GAK Plama. /// TOOLS: Photoshop, Flash, XML. /// COST: 100 hours.

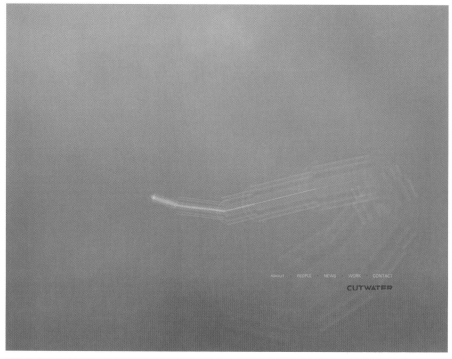

Info

DESIGN STUDIO: Gringo <www.gringo.nu>. /// **DESIGN:** Gringo. /// **PROGRAMMING:** Gringo. /// **CONTENTS:** Motion-graphics, music, text, photo. /// **TYPE:** Digital agency. /// **CLIENT:** Cutwater. /// **TOOLS:** Photoshop, Illustrator, HTML, XML, Flash, Maya, Database editor, Final Cut Pro, After Effects. /// **COST:** 45 days.

DESIGN STUDIO: Daniël Sytsma <www.danielsytsma.nl>. /// **DESIGN:** Daniël Sytsma. /// **PROGRAMMING:** Simon Hattinga Verschure. /// **CONTENTS:** Illustration, photo, text. /// **TYPE:** Designer. /// **TOOLS:** Flash, Illustrator, XML, HTML, PHP. /// **AWARDS:** Fcukstar. /// **COST:** 80 hours.

Info

Daniel
Zimmerman
Music for film
& tv
_News_Music_Bio_Contact

Upgrade
Project: LG
"The beauty of breaking with
your past."
—*listen*

Daniel
Zimmerman
Music for film
& tv
_News_Music_Bio_Contact

track:	project:	genre:
Sammy Gets Caught	Botero in Blue	Dark Comedy
Botero Gives Chase	Botero in Blue	Dark Comedy
Simple and Sad	Botero in Blue	Dark Comedy
Last Call	Botero in Blue	Dark Comedy
Analog Binge	Forever Neon	Commercial
Nowhere Planned	In Memory of Spring	Drama
You'd See You	Volvo c30	Commercial
Swoon	Volvo c30	Commercial
Ricky Gonna Bring It	Michael and Ricky	Comedy
Tag Team	Michael and Ricky	Comedy
Driven to Boredom	Office Party	Comedy
Magical Stapler	Office Party	Comedy
Catharsis	Hockey in Empty Pools	Drama
Down in Chinatown	Down in Chinatown	Commercial
Can't You Just Feel the Love	Family of the Year (Pilot)	Comedy
What a Lovely Family	Family of the Year (Pilot)	Comedy

Info

DESIGN STUDIO: Loyal Design <www.thisisloyal.com>. /// DESIGN: Loyal Design. /// PROGRAMMING: Loyal Design. /// CONTENTS: Music. ///
TYPE: Composer. /// CLIENT: Daniel Zimmerman. /// TOOLS: Photoshop, Flash, HTML, PHP. /// COST: 440 hours.

DANKA STUDIO

www.dankastudio.fr

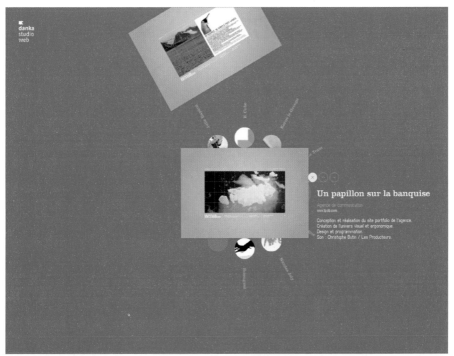

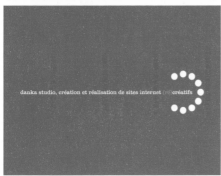

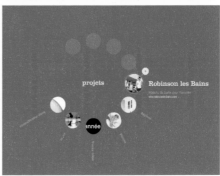

Info

DESIGN STUDIO: Danka Studio <www.dankastudio.fr>. /// DESIGN: Guillaume Bonnecase. /// PROGRAMMING: Grégoire Gérardin, Vincent Perrier-Perrery. /// CONTENTS: Photo, text. /// TYPE: Web design studio. /// TOOLS: Photoshop, Flash, XML, PHP. /// AWARDS: DesignCharts. /// COST: 100–150 hours.

Info

DESIGN STUDIO: Dimomedia Lab <www.dimomedia.com>. /// DESIGN: Massimo Sirelli, Valentina Garlant. /// PROGRAMMING: Massimo Sirelli, Fabrizio Simeoni, Fabrizio Parodi. /// CONTENTS: Photo. /// TYPE: Photographer. /// CLIENT: Daylight Studio. /// TOOLS: Flash, XML.

DESIGN STUDIO: Aer visual studio <www.aerstudio.com>. /// DESIGN: Aer studio. /// PROGRAMMING: Aer studio. /// CONTENTS: Photo. /// TYPE: Product design company. /// CLIENT: Design Code. /// TOOLS: Flash, XML, PHP, HTML, Illustrator. /// AWARDS: ADG-FAD Laus Awards. /// COST: 180 hours.

Info

DESIGN STUDIO: Simone Inc. <www.ilovesimone.com>. /// **DESIGN:** Kaie Murakami (Art Direction); Sin Masuda. /// **PROGRAMMING:** Sin Masuda. ///
CONTENTS: Photo. /// **TYPE:** Sunglasses brand. /// **CLIENT:** Dita. /// **TOOLS:** Flash, XML. /// **COST:** 50 hours.

Info

DESIGN STUDIO: Dimomedia Lab <www.dimomedia.com>. /// **DESIGN:** Massimo Sirelli, Valentina Garlant. /// **PROGRAMMING:** Massimo Sirelli, Fabrizio Parodi. /// **CONTENTS:** Text, photo, music. /// **TYPE:** DJ. /// **CLIENT:** DJ Double S. /// **TOOLS:** Flash, XML. /// **AWARDS:** Internet Vibes, pages.blueidea.com, e-Creative, Produce Media, europeanwebaward.com, Robocore, Web Design Library, visualdesigner.net, PixelMakers.

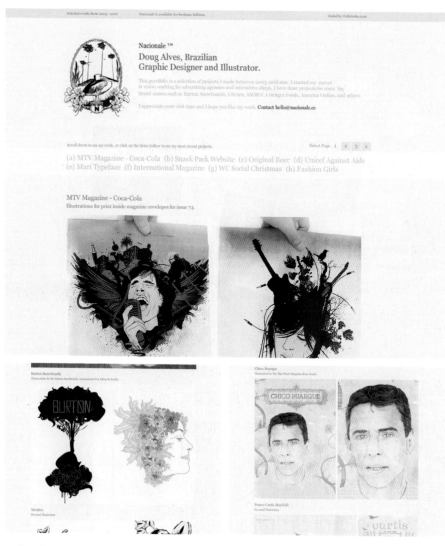

Info DESIGN STUDIO: Nacionale <www.nacionale.cc>. /// DESIGN: Doug Alves, Keita kun. /// PROGRAMMING: Keita Kun. /// CONTENTS: Photo, illustration, text. /// TYPE: Graphic artist and illustrator. /// TOOLS: Photoshop, Illustrator, Flash.

DESIGN STUDIO: DrawingArt <www.drawingart.org>. /// **DESIGN:** Miro Koljanin. /// **PROGRAMMING:** Miro Koljanin. /// **CONTENTS:** Photo, illustration, text. /// **TYPE:** Design and development studio. /// **TOOLS:** Photoshop, Flash, XML, HTML, PHP. /// **AWARDS:** FWA (Site of the Day), DOPE Awards, The Dreamer, Fcukstar, Web Design Awards, Design Licks, Creative Website Awards.

DURAS AMBIENT

www.duras-ambient.com

Info

DESIGN STUDIO: Simone Inc. <www.ilovesimone.com>. /// **DESIGN:** Kaie Murakami (Art Direction); Tatsuya Masumura. /// **PROGRAMMING:** Tatsuya Masumura. /// **CONTENTS:** Photo. /// **TYPE:** Fashion brand. /// **CLIENT:** Duras Inc. /// **TOOLS:** Flash, XML, Photoshop. /// **COST:** 100 hours.

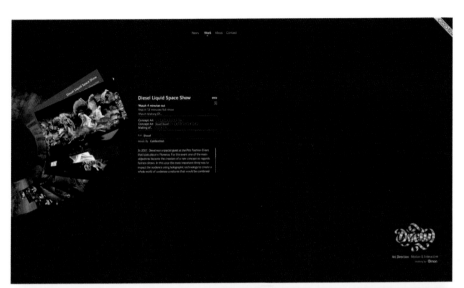

Info

DESIGN STUDIO: Dvein <www.dvein.com>. /// **DESIGN:** Carlos Pardo, Teo Guillem, Fernando Dominguez. /// **PROGRAMMING:** Carlos Pardo. /// **CONTENTS:** Motion-graphics, photo. /// **TYPE:** Motion and interactive studio. /// **TOOLS:** Flash, Flex, Photoshop. /// **AWARDS:** FWA (Site of the Day), Creative Website Awards. /// **COST:** 200 hours.

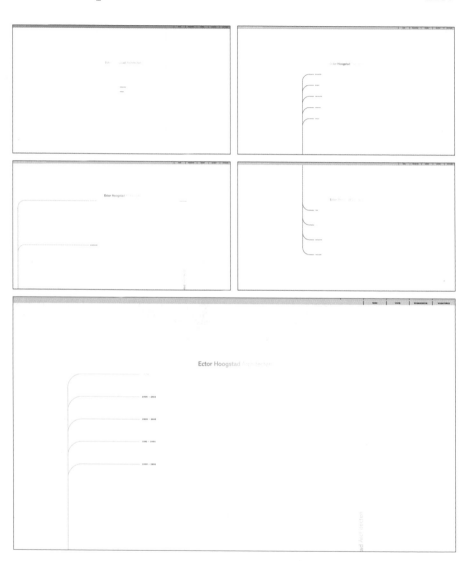

Info

DESIGN STUDIO: DC <www.dcworks.nl>. /// **DESIGN:** Martijn Rietveld, Maarten Mieras. /// **PROGRAMMING:** Michiel Sikma. /// **CONTENTS:** Photo, illustration, text. /// **TYPE:** Architecture studio. /// **CLIENT:** Ector Hoogstad. /// **TOOLS:** Flash, XML. /// **COST:** 400 hours.

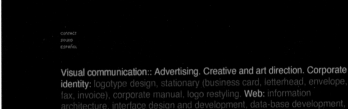

Visual communication:: Advertising. Creative and art direction. Corporate
identity: logotype design, stationary (business card, letterhead, envelope,
fax, invoice), corporate manual, logo restyling. Web: information
architecture, interface design and development, data-base development,
back-office, online store, online video, search engine optimization, flash,
html, php, asp. Print: magazine, book, corporate brochure, annual report,
catalogue, packaging, poster, signage. Motion graphics. Photography::
Architecture, Studio, Portrait. Product design. Interior design

Info

DESIGN STUDIO: elespacio <www.elespacio.net>. /// DESIGN: Juanmi Sansinenea, Agnieszka Sekreta, Iker Iturria. /// PROGRAMMING: Juanmi
Sansinenea; Xavi Pujol. /// CONTENTS: Photo, illustration, text. /// TYPE: Design Studio. /// TOOLS: Photoshop, Flash.

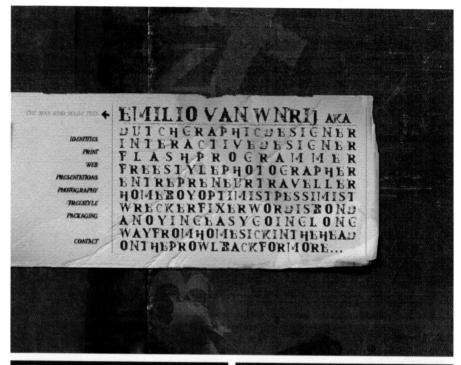

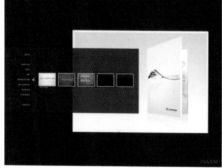

Info DESIGN STUDIO: GAZZ <www.gazz.nl>. /// DESIGN: Emilio van Wanrooij. /// PROGRAMMING: Emilio van Wanrooij. /// CONTENTS: Photo, text. ///
TYPE: Designer. /// TOOLS: Flash.

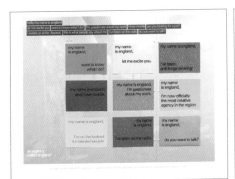

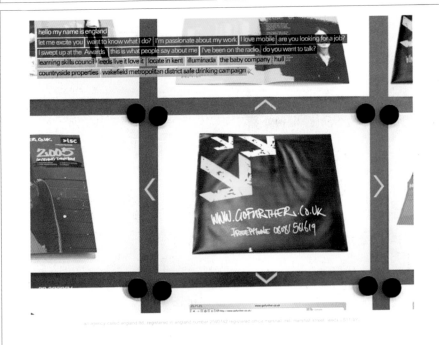

Info

DESIGN STUDIO: An Agency Called England <www.englandagency.com>. /// **DESIGN:** Martin Pownall (Head of Interactive); Paul Alexander (Creative Director); Ross Featherstone. /// **PROGRAMMING:** Oliver Dore, Mark Strofton. /// **CONTENTS:** Photo, text. /// **TYPE:** Advertising, design, interactive, mobile, PR, and media buying. /// **TOOLS:** Photoshop, Illustrator, FreeHand, Flash. /// **COST:** 100 hours.

ENRICO PELLIZZONI

www.enricopellizzoni.com

Info

DESIGN STUDIO: Vergani & Gasco <www.technemedia.it>. /// **DESIGN:** Luigi Vergani, Nicola Gasco. /// **PROGRAMMING:** Luigi Vergani, Nicola Gasco. ///
CONTENTS: Photo, text. /// **TYPE:** Leather furniture design. /// **CLIENT:** Enrico Pellizzoni S.r.l. /// **TOOLS:** Flash, XML, PHP, MySQL, Photoshop. ///
AWARDS: Netdiver, Website Design Awards, e-Creative, Faveup, Mowsnet, gouw.nu, Xhilarate, Spyline, N229, Linkage. /// **COST:** 6 weeks.

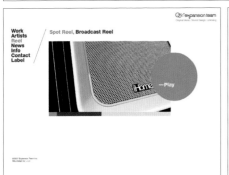

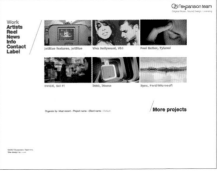

Info

DESIGN STUDIO: Loyal Design <www.thisisloyal.com>. /// DESIGN: Loyal Design. /// PROGRAMMING: Loyal Design. /// CONTENTS: Video, music. ///
TYPE: Composers, producers, musicians and DJs. /// CLIENT: Expansion Team. /// TOOLS: Photoshop, Flash, HTML, PHP. /// COST: 480 hours.

FABIO LANA

www.fabiolana.com

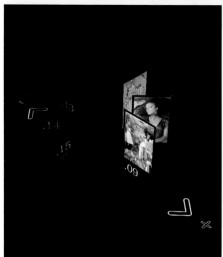

Info

DESIGN STUDIO: Gabriele Vinci <www.gabrielevinci.com>. /// **DESIGN:** Gabriele Vinci. /// **PROGRAMMING:** Gabriele Vinci. /// **CONTENTS:** Photo. ///
TYPE: Photographer. /// **CLIENT:** Fabio Lana. /// **TOOLS:** Papervision, Flash, XML. /// **AWARDS:** FWA (Site of the Day), Art Directors Club Italy (Winner).
/// **COST:** 2 weeks.

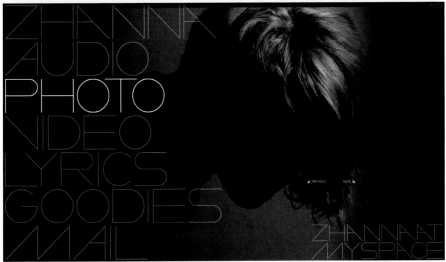

Info

DESIGN STUDIO: area3 <www.area3.net>. /// **DESIGN:** Sebastián Puiggrós, Chema Longobardo. /// **PROGRAMMING:** Federico Joselevich. /// **CONTENTS:** Music, video, text, photo. /// **TYPE:** Electronic musician. /// **CLIENT:** Zhanna. /// **TOOLS:** Flash. /// **COST:** 3 months.

Info DESIGN STUDIO: Andy Foulds Design <www.andyfoulds.co.uk>. /// DESIGN: Andy Foulds. /// PROGRAMMING: Andy Foulds. /// CONTENTS: Music, video, text, photo. /// TYPE: Film and TV special-effects costume company. /// CLIENT: FBFX. /// TOOLS: Flash, HTML, Photoshop, Homesite. /// AWARDS: Flashforward, FWA, Ultrashock Bomshock, Macromedia (Site of the Day). /// COST: 220 hours.

Info

DESIGN STUDIO: Mkt Virtual <www.mktvirtual.com.br>. /// DESIGN: Ludmilla Rossi, André Pires. /// PROGRAMMING: André Pires. /// CONTENTS: Music, video, text, photo. /// TYPE: Advertising agency. /// CLIENT: Fenômeno Propaganda. /// TOOLS: Flash, XML. /// AWARDS: FestMultimídia (Institutional Website), The Dreamer, PixelMakers. /// COST: 160 hours.

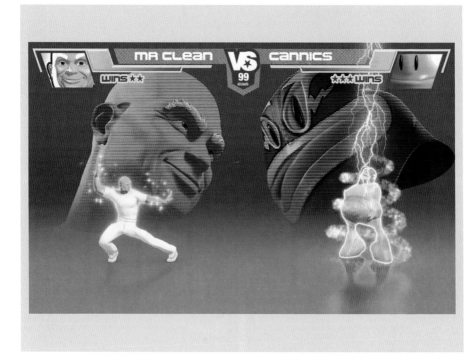

Info

DESIGN STUDIO: 3deluxe motion <www.3deluxe.de>. /// **DESIGN:** 3deluxe motion: Sascha Koeth, Stephan Lauhoff (Design/Concept); Fiftyeight 3d: Max Zimmermann (3d Animaton). /// **PROGRAMMING:** 3deluxe motion. /// **CONTENTS:** Music, video, text, illustration, photo. /// **TYPE:** 3d character design studio. /// **CLIENT:** Fiftyeight 3d Animation & Digital Effects GmbH. /// **TOOLS:** Flash, After Effects, Softimage, Cinema 4D, Photoshop, Illustrator. /// **AWARDS:** iF Design, Red Dot Design Award, FWA. /// **COST:** 6 months.

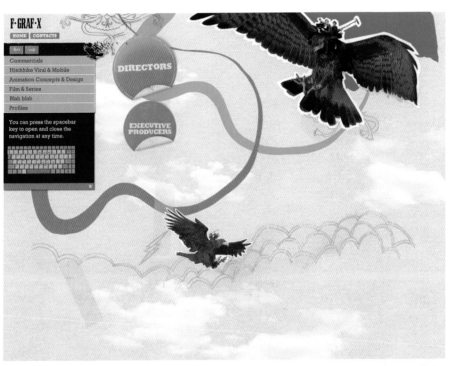

Info
DESIGN STUDIO: Resn Creative <www.resn.co.nz>. /// DESIGN: Resn Creative. /// PROGRAMMING: Resn Creative. /// CONTENTS: Video, illustration, animation, photo, text. /// TYPE: Production company. /// CLIENT: Filmgraphics. /// TOOLS: Flash, Photoshop, MySQL, PHP, Notepad. /// COST: 5 weeks.

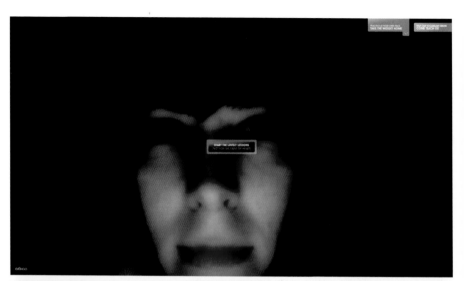

Info DESIGN STUDIO: Gringo <www.gringo.nu>. /// DESIGN: Gringo. /// PROGRAMMING: Gringo. /// CONTENTS: Music, video. /// TYPE: Digital agency. ///
TOOLS: Photoshop, Illustrator, HTML, XML, Flash, Maya, Database editor, Final Cut Pro, After Effects. /// AWARDS: Wave Festival. /// COST: 60 days.

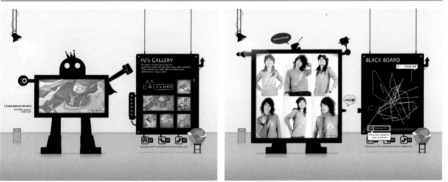

DESIGN STUDIO: fu-design.com <www.fu-design.com>. /// **DESIGN:** fu-design.com. /// **PROGRAMMING:** fu-design.com. /// **CONTENTS:** illustration, music, animation, video. /// **TYPE:** Illustrator. /// **TOOLS:** Flash, Photoshop, ASP, Fruitloop, Dreamweaver. /// **AWARDS:** FWA, Webby Nominees. /// **COST:** 6 months.

GEORGE KHMALADZE
ARCHITECT / PERSONAL PORTFOLIO

Entertainment center
2007

1st PRIZE WINNER. Competition held by "Bagebey City Group". Subject of competition: multifunctional entertainment complex in Batumi, seaside city in Georgia. Including cafe bars with terraces on different levels with panoramic view towards the sea, restaurant, nightclub, cinema, amphitheatre, multi-use space, swimming pool & fitness center.

TYPE: Competition / personal project.

GEORGE KHMALADZE
ARCHITECT / PERSONAL PORTFOLIO

Russian orthodox church

Business center
2003

Info

DESIGN STUDIO: Pixel <www.pixel.ge>. /// **DESIGN:** George Khmaladze. /// **PROGRAMMING:** George Marnadze. /// **CONTENTS:** Photo. /// **TYPE:** Architecture company. /// **CLIENT:** George Khmaladze. /// **TOOLS:** Flash, XML. /// **COST:** 2 weeks.

Info

DESIGN STUDIO: 3indesign Media Solutions <www.3indesign.com>. /// **DESIGN:** Pablo Vega Correa, Edgar Francisco Solano Chávez, Ricardo Espinosa Trejo. /// **PROGRAMMING:** Pablo Vega Correa, Edgar Francisco Solano Chávez. /// **CONTENTS:** Illustration, animation, photo. /// **TYPE:** Architectonic developments. /// **CLIENT:** GFA Architects. /// **TOOLS:** Photoshop, Flash, After Effects. /// **COST:** 620 hours.

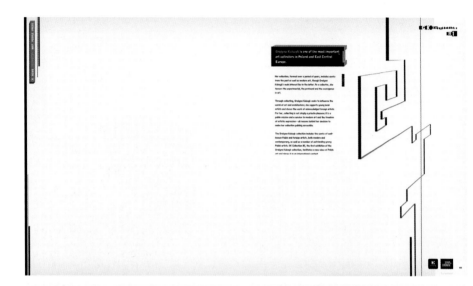

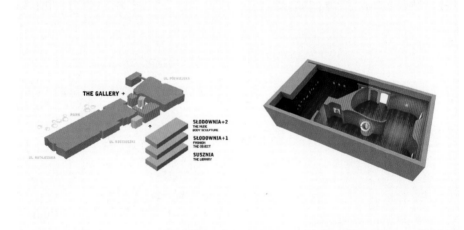

Info

DESIGN STUDIO: Huncwot <www.huncwot.com>. /// **DESIGN:** Lukasz Knasiecki, Arek Romanski. /// **PROGRAMMING:** Lukasz Knasiecki, Arek Romanski. /// **CONTENTS:** Photo. /// **TYPE:** Art collection. /// **CLIENT:** Kulczyk Foundation. /// **TOOLS:** 3d Studio Max, Freehand, Photoshop, Flash, PHP/SQL. /// **COST:** 160 hours.

COW PARADE RIO
ILLUSTRATION : 2007

Info

DESIGN STUDIO: Glauco Diogenes Studio <www.glaucodiogenes.com.br>. /// **DESIGN:** Glauco Diogenes. /// **PROGRAMMING:** José Fernando Carneiro "Zeh". /// **CONTENTS:** Photo. /// **TYPE:** Designer. /// **TOOLS:** Flash, Photoshop, Freehand. /// **COST:** US$ 3,000.

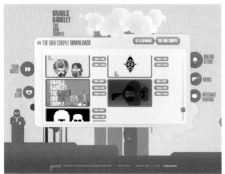

DESIGN STUDIO: Rokkan <www.rokkan.com>. /// **DESIGN:** John Noe, John Gist. /// **PROGRAMMING:** Akeem Philbert, Beep Iams, Andy Prondak, Pau Collins. /// **CONTENTS:** Video, photo, text. /// **TYPE:** Musician. /// **CLIENT:** Atlantic Records. /// **TOOLS:** Flash, Photoshop, Illustrator. /// **COST:** 400 hours.

GOANNA WEBDESIGN

www.goanna-webdesign.com

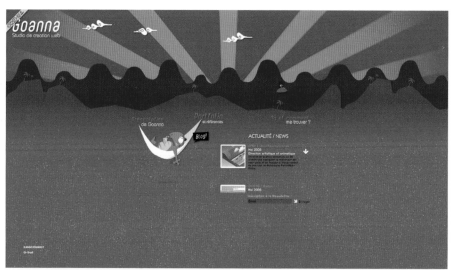

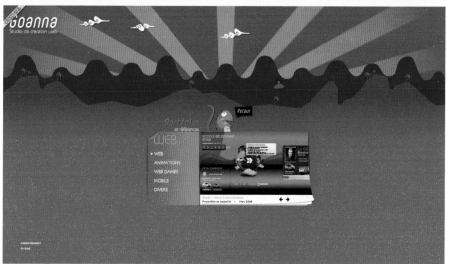

Info

DESIGN STUDIO: Studio Goanna <www.goanna-webdesign.com>. /// **DESIGN:** Stéphane Munnier. /// **PROGRAMMING:** Stéphane Munnier. /// **CONTENTS:** Video, illustration, animation, photo, text. /// **TYPE:** Flash designer. /// **TOOLS:** Flash. /// **AWARDS:** FWA. /// **COST:** 120 hours.

Info

DESIGN STUDIO: Grand Creative <www.wearegrand.com>. /// **DESIGN:** Luke Canning. /// **PROGRAMMING:** Matthew Quinn. /// **CONTENTS:** Photo, text. /// **TYPE:** Design studio. /// **TOOLS:** Photoshop, Illustrator, Flash, Coda, Transmit.

Info

DESIGN STUDIO: Hello Monday <www.hellomonday.com>. /// **DESIGN:** Hello Monday. /// **PROGRAMMING:** Hello Monday. /// **CONTENTS:** Video, photo, text. /// **TYPE:** Fashion brand. /// **CLIENT:** Gudrun & Gudrun. /// **TOOLS:** Flash, Flex, XML, PHP, Photoshop, Premiere. /// **AWARDS:** FWA (Site of the Day), NewWebPick, Fcukstar, DesignCharts, Communication Arts. /// **COST:** 150 hours.

Info

DESIGN STUDIO: multimediaHAAM <www.multimediahaam.com>; Guy Sealey <www.guysealey.com>. /// **DESIGN:** Guy Sealey, Aragorn Ligocki. ///
PROGRAMMING: Guy Sealey, Aragorn Ligocki. /// **CONTENTS:** Video, illustration, animation, photo, text. /// **TYPE:** Creative Director. /// **CLIENT:**
Guy Sealey. /// **TOOLS:** Flash, ActionScript, Illustrator.

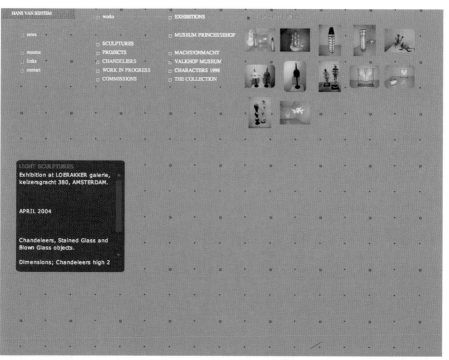

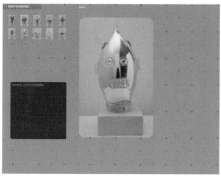
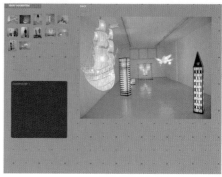

Info

DESIGN STUDIO: DC <www.dcworks.nl>. /// DESIGN: Merijn van Essen, Martijn Rietveld. /// PROGRAMMING: Merijn van Essen. /// CONTENTS: Photo, text. /// TYPE: Artist and sculptor. /// CLIENT: Hans van Bentem. /// TOOLS: Flash, XML. /// COST: 180 hours.

HELLOHELLO!!

www.hellohello.bz

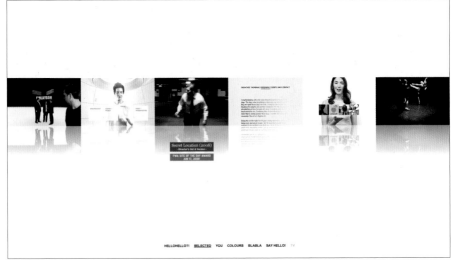

DESIGN STUDIO: HELLOHELLO!! <www.hellohello.bz>. /// **DESIGN:** Thierry Loa "Dr. Hello". /// **PROGRAMMING:** Thierry Loa "Dr. Hello". /// **CONTENTS:** Video, illustration, animation, photo, text. /// **TYPE:** Creative and production house. /// **TOOLS:** Flash, Premiere, Photoshop, HTML. /// **COST:** 2 weeks.

HELLOHIKIMORI

www.hellohikimori.com

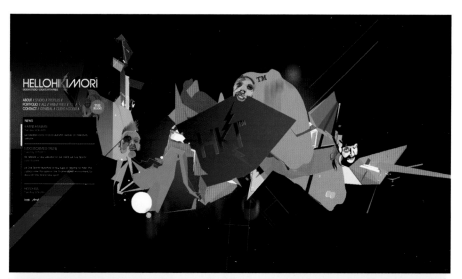

Info

DESIGN STUDIO: Hellohikimori <www.hellohikimori.com>. /// **DESIGN:** David Rondel Cambou. /// **PROGRAMMING:** Vincent Legrand. /// **CONTENTS:** Photo, illustration, text. /// **TYPE:** Design Agency. /// **TOOLS:** Flash. /// **AWARDS:** FWA (Site of the Day). /// **COST:** 100 hours.

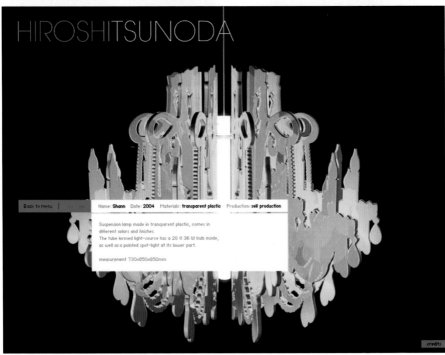

Info

DESIGN STUDIO: Aer visual studio <www.aerstudio.com>. /// DESIGN: Aer studio. /// PROGRAMMING: Aer studio. /// CONTENTS: Photo, illustration, text. /// TYPE: Product design studio. /// CLIENT: Hiroshi Tsunoda Design Studio. /// TOOLS: Flash, XML, HTML, PHP, Illustrator. /// AWARDS: ADG-FAD Laus Awards. /// COST: 180 hours.

Info

DESIGN STUDIO: hotmonkey design <www.hotmonkeydesign.com>. /// DESIGN: hotmonkey design; quickyboy: Mihai Bogdan. /// PROGRAMMING: quickyboy: Mihai Bogdan; hotmonkey design. /// CONTENTS: Illustration, photo, text. /// TYPE: Design studio. /// TOOLS: Photoshop, Flash, XML, HTML. /// COST: 4–6 weeks.

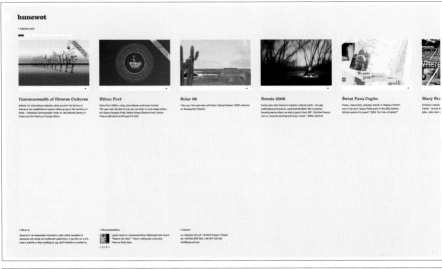

DESIGN STUDIO: Huncwot <www.huncwot.com>. /// **DESIGN:** Arek Romanski, Lukasz Knasiecki. /// **PROGRAMMING:** Arek Romanski, Lukasz Knasiecki. /// **CONTENTS:** Video, illustration, animation, photo, text. /// **TYPE:** Interactive design studio. /// **TOOLS:** Photoshop, Flash (ActionScript). /// **COST:** 10 hours.

Info   **DESIGN STUDIO:** Ideasamedida <www.ideasamedida.com>. /// **DESIGN:** Pablo Feldman, Pablo Lewin, Gustavo Reinoso. /// **PROGRAMMING:** Ideasamedida. /// **CONTENTS:** Illustration, photo, text. /// **TYPE:** Design Studio. /// **TOOLS:** Flash, HTML. /// **COST:** 200 hours.

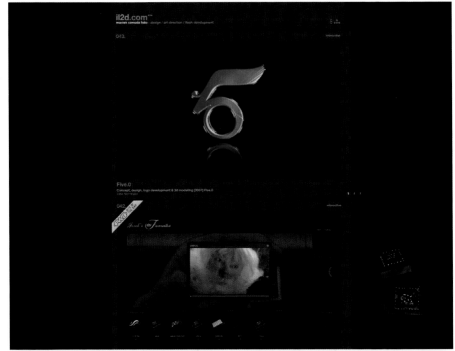

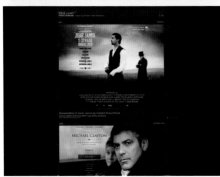

Info

DESIGN STUDIO: il2d.com <www.il2d.com>. /// **DESIGN:** Maciek Czmuda. /// **PROGRAMMING:** Maciek Czmuda. /// **CONTENTS:** Animation, text, photo. /// **TYPE:** Designer. /// **TOOLS:** Photoshop, Flash. /// **COST:** 120 hours.

IMAGE MOVERS DIGITAL

www.imagemoversdigital.com

Info

DESIGN STUDIO: Openfield Creative <www.openfieldcreative.com>. /// **DESIGN:** Brandon Blangger, Brian Keenan (Creative Direction); Josh Barnes (Strategy Director). /// **CONTENTS:** Video, illustration, animation, photo, text. /// **TYPE:** 3d animation and motion capture film studio. /// **CLIENT:** Image Movers Digital. /// **TOOLS:** Flash, AS2, XML, Photoshop, Illustrator. /// **AWARDS:** FWA (Site of the Day), DOPE Awards. /// **COST:** 175 hours.

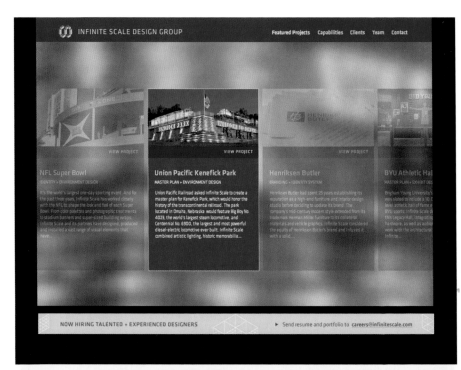

Info

DESIGN STUDIO: Openfield Creative <www.openfieldcreative.com>. /// DESIGN: Brandon Blangger, Brian Keenan (Creative Direction); Josh Barnes (Strategy Director). /// CONTENTS: Illustration, photo, text. /// TYPE: Branding and environmental graphic design studio. /// CLIENT: Infinite Scale Design Group. /// TOOLS: Flash, AS2, XML, Photoshop, Illustrator. /// COST: 90 hours.

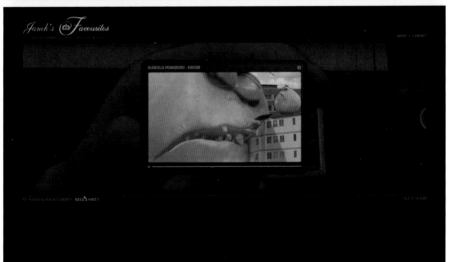

Info

DESIGN STUDIO: il2d.com <www.il2d.com>. /// DESIGN: Maciek Czmuda. /// PROGRAMMING: Jakub Matuszewski. /// CONTENTS: Movies, animations. /// TYPE: Entertainment and movie production studio. /// CLIENT: Janek's Favourites. /// TOOLS: Photoshop, Flash, After Effects. /// AWARDS: FWA (Site of the Day). /// COST: 160 hours.

JESÚS VILAMAJÓ

www.vilamajo.com

Design Studio: Aer visual studio <www.aerstudio.com>. /// **Design:** Aer studio. /// **Programming:** Aer studio. /// **Contents:** Photo. ///
Type: Photographer. /// **Client:** Jesús Vilamajó. /// **Tools:** Flash, Illustrator, XML, HTML, PHP, MySQL. /// **Awards:** ADG-FAD Laus Awards. ///
Cost: 320 hours.

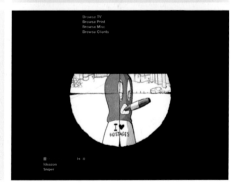

Info

DESIGN STUDIO: HELLOHELLO!! <www.hellohello.bz>. /// **DESIGN:** Thierry Loa "Dr. Hello" (Creative/Audio/Video/Design). /// **PROGRAMMING:** Thierry Loa "Dr. Hello", Nolan Dubeau. /// **CONTENTS:** Animation, text, illustration, photo. /// **TYPE:** Advertising agency. /// **CLIENT:** john st. Advertising Agency. /// **TOOLS:** Flash, Premiere, Sound Forge, Coldfusion. /// **AWARDS:** FWA (Site of the Day), ADCC (Gold). /// **COST:** 10 weeks.

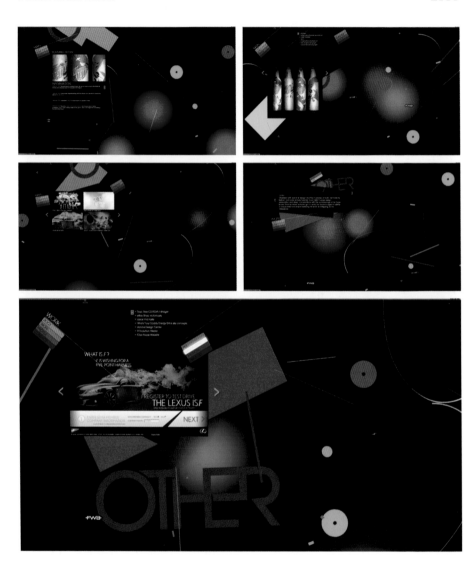

Info

DESIGN STUDIO: Othra <www.othdsn.com>. /// **DESIGN:** Jozias Dawson. /// **PROGRAMMING:** Jozias Dawson. /// **CONTENTS:** Video, illustration, animation, photo, text. /// **TYPE:** Creative Director. /// **TOOLS:** Flash, Illustrator, Photoshop. /// **AWARDS:** FWA. /// **COST:** 160 hours.

Info

DESIGN STUDIO: 21TORR Agency GmbH <www.21torr.com>. /// DESIGN: Klaus Grotz (Art Direction); Marion Stolz. /// PROGRAMMING: Andreas Bauer. /// CONTENTS: Photo, text. /// TYPE: Architecture studio. /// CLIENT: JSK Dipl. Ing. Architekten. /// TOOLS: Flash, MySQL, PHP, XML. /// AWARDS: Jahrbuch der Werbung, iF Communication Design Award, Deutscher Multimedia Award (Nominee), FWA, Mowsnet, DOPE Awards.

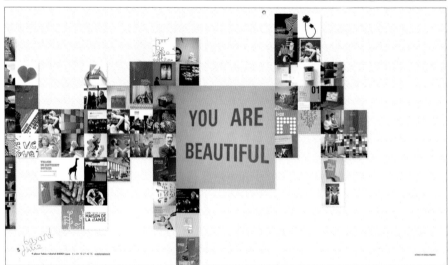

Info

DESIGN STUDIO: Danka Studio <www.dankastudio.fr>. /// DESIGN: Guillaume Bonnecase, Grégoire Gérardin. /// PROGRAMMING: Grégoire Gérardin. /// CONTENTS: Photo, illustration, text. /// TYPE: Art director and designer. /// CLIENT: Julie Bayard. /// TOOLS: Photoshop, Flash, XML, PHP. /// COST: 150–200 hours.

Info

DESIGN STUDIO: OnClick Studio <www.onclick.es>. /// **DESIGN:** Ramon del Nozal, Iosu Luengo, Alex Albizu. /// **PROGRAMMING:** Ramon del Nozal, Iosu Luengo, Alex Albizu. /// **CONTENTS:** Photo, illustration, text. /// **TYPE:** Advertising agency. /// **CLIENT:** LaLuca Comunicación. /// **TOOLS:** Flash, Photoshop, Illustrator. /// **COST:** 200 hours.

L'ÂMOSCOPE

www.lamoscope.org

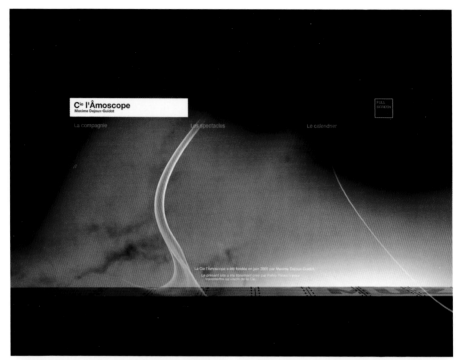

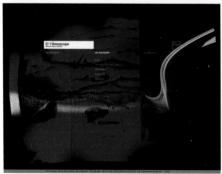

Info

DESIGN STUDIO: nanozoom <www.nanozoom.net>. /// **DESIGN:** Pablo Pinasco; Christophe Menassier (Sound Design). /// **PROGRAMMING:** Pablo Pinasco. /// **CONTENTS:** Music, text, illustration, photo. /// **TYPE:** Theather company. /// **CLIENT:** L'Âmoscope Maxime Dejoux. /// **TOOLS:** Flash, Fireworks, Photoshop, Dreamweaver. /// **COST:** 160 hours.

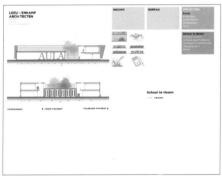

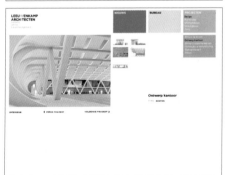

Info

DESIGN STUDIO: DC <www.dcworks.nl>. /// DESIGN: Martijn Rietveld, Merijn van Essen. /// PROGRAMMING: Merijn van Essen. /// CONTENTS: Photo, text. /// TYPE: Architecture studio. /// CLIENT: Leeuwenkamp Architects; Shop Around. /// TOOLS: Flash, XML. /// COST: 200 hours.

DESIGN STUDIO: Medusateam <www.medusateam.com>. /// DESIGN: Medusateam. /// PROGRAMMING: Medusateam. /// CONTENTS: Illustration, animation, photo. /// TYPE: Design Agency. /// CLIENT: Legend. /// TOOLS: Flash, Photoshop, Illustrator, XML, HTML, PHP/MySQL. /// COST: 250 hours.

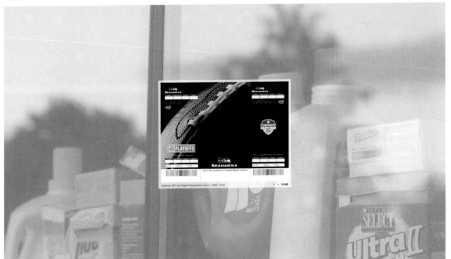

Design Studio: Revolver Creative <www.revolvercreative.com>. /// **Design:** Matthew Fordham. /// **Programming:** Matthew Fordham. /// **Contents:** Video, illustration, animation, photo, text. /// **Type:** Advertising agency. /// **Client:** Levy LLC. /// **Tools:** Flash, Photoshop, XML, PHP, MySQL. /// **Cost:** 60 hours.

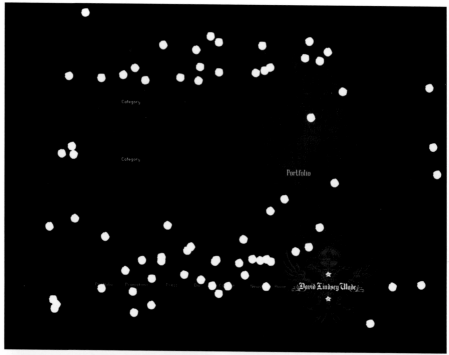

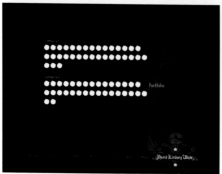

DESIGN STUDIO: Hello Monday <www.hellomonday.com>. /// **DESIGN:** Hello Monday. /// **PROGRAMMING:** Hello Monday. /// **CONTENTS:** Photo, text. ///
TYPE: Photographer. /// **CLIENT:** Lindsey Wade. /// **TOOLS:** Flash, Flex, XML, PHP, Photoshop. /// **COST:** 150 hours.

Info

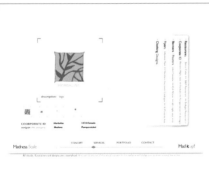
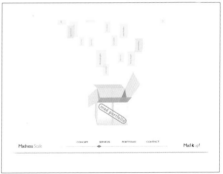

Info

DESIGN STUDIO: Nobrand <www.nobrand.name>. /// DESIGN: Badeeh Abla (Art Director); Enas Mtaweh (Junior Designer). /// PROGRAMMING: Rabeeh Abla (Software Architect); Saleem Badreddine (Junior Programmer). /// CONTENTS: Photo, illustration, text. /// TYPE: Advertising agency. /// CLIENT: Mad Design. /// TOOLS: XML, PHP, Flash, Photoshop. /// COST: 240 hours.

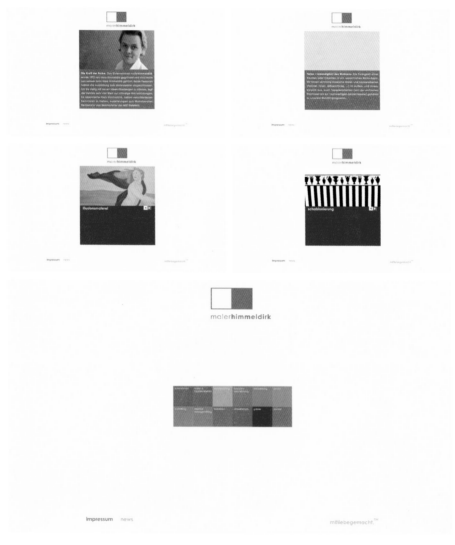

DESIGN STUDIO: Nalindesign <www.nalindesign.com>. /// **DESIGN:** Michaela Duisberg, Andre Weier. /// **PROGRAMMING:** Andre Weier. /// **CONTENTS:** Photo, text. /// **TYPE:** Painter. /// **CLIENT:** Maler Himmeldirk. /// **TOOLS:** Flash, Photoshop, HTML. /// **AWARDS:** NewWebPick, Web Design Index 7, Web Design Library (Site of the Day), e-Creative (Site of the Day). /// **COST:** 3 months.

Info

DESIGN STUDIO: mediaBOOM <www.mediaBOOM.com>. /// **DESIGN:** mediaBOOM. /// **PROGRAMMING:** mediaBOOM. /// **CONTENTS:** Photo, animation, illustration, text. /// **TYPE:** Interactive agency. /// **TOOLS:** Flash, HTML, Photoshop, After Effects, Maya. /// **AWARDS:** Webby Awards (Best Professional Website), Pixel Awards (Best in Show), FWA (Site of the Day), Connecticut Art Directors Club (Best in Show). /// **COST:** 500 hours.

DESIGN STUDIO: Medusateam <www.medusateam.com>. /// **DESIGN:** Medusateam. /// **PROGRAMMING:** Medusateam. /// **CONTENTS:** Illustration, animation, photo, text. /// **TYPE:** Design agency. /// **TOOLS:** Flash, Photoshop, Illustrator, XML, HTML, PHP/MySQL. /// **COST:** 180 hours.

Info

DESIGN STUDIO: Huncwot <www.huncwot.com>. /// **DESIGN:** Arek Romanski, Lukasz Knasiecki. /// **PROGRAMMING:** Arek Romanski, Lukasz Knasiecki. /// **CONTENTS:** Music, text, illustration, photo. /// **TYPE:** Outdoor media agency. /// **CLIENT:** Metropolis. /// **TOOLS:** Photoshop, Flash (ActionScript), MySQL/PHP. /// **AWARDS:** FWA (Site of the Day). /// **COST:** 150 hours.

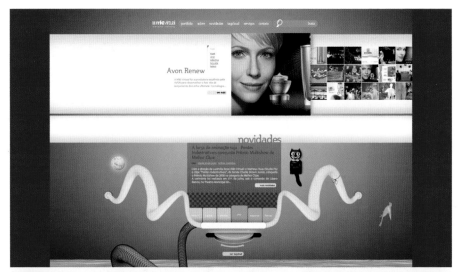

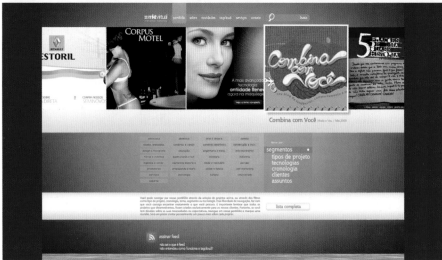

Info

DESIGN STUDIO: Mkt Virtual <www.mktvirtual.com.br>. /// **DESIGN:** Ludmilla Rossi, Niva Silva. /// **PROGRAMMING:** Rodrigo Moyle, Danilo Costa, Gabriel Caires, Guilherme Almeida. /// **CONTENTS:** Illustration, animation, motion-graphics, music, photo. /// **TYPE:** Interactive agency. /// **TOOLS:** Flash, Wordpress integrated with Flash, XML, CakePHP. /// **COST:** 390 hours.

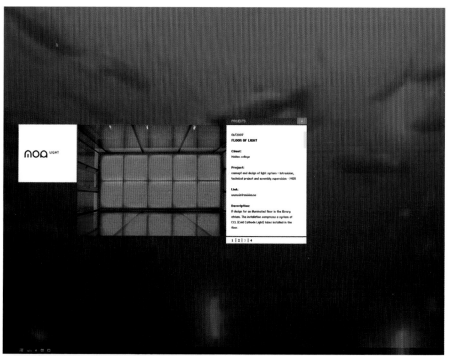

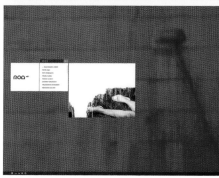

Info

DESIGN STUDIO: Huncwot <www.huncwot.com>. /// DESIGN: Lukasz Knasiecki, Arek Romanski. /// PROGRAMMING: Lukasz Knasiecki, Arek Romanski. /// CONTENTS: Photo, text. /// TYPE: Design studio. /// CLIENT: Moa. /// TOOLS: Photoshop, Flash (ActionScript), PHP/SQL. /// COST: 120 hours.

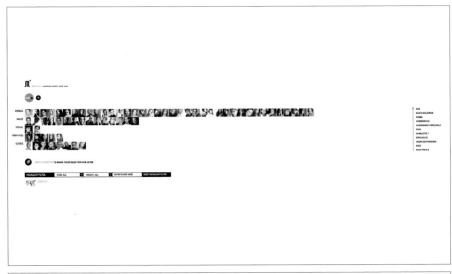

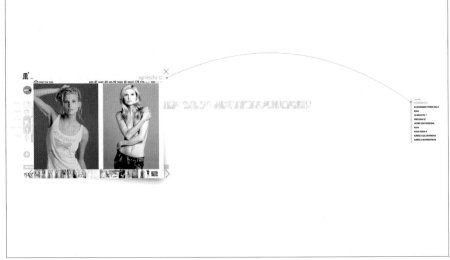

DESIGN STUDIO: il2d.com <www.il2d.com>. /// **DESIGN:** Maciek Czmuda. /// **PROGRAMMING:** Jakub Matuszewski. /// **CONTENTS:** Photo, text. /// **TYPE:** Fashion, modeling and entertainment studio. /// **CLIENT:** Modelplus. /// **TOOLS:** Photoshop, Flash, After Effects. /// **COST:** 150 hours.

Info

DESIGN STUDIO: Strange <www.strangecorp.com>. /// **DESIGN:** Jamie Sergeant, Nick Bain. /// **PROGRAMMING:** Ricardo Sanchez, John Parker. /// **CONTENTS:** Photo, text. /// **TYPE:** Furniture designers. /// **CLIENT:** Morgan Design. /// **TOOLS:** Illustrator, Photoshop, Flash, PHP, XML, HTML. /// **COST:** 90 Hours.

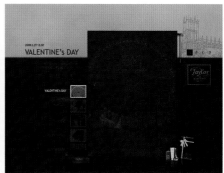

Info

DESIGN STUDIO: fu-design.com <www.fu-design.com>. /// CONTENTS: Photo, text. /// TYPE: Merchandise promotion. /// TOOLS: Flash, Photoshop, ASP. /// COST: 2 months.

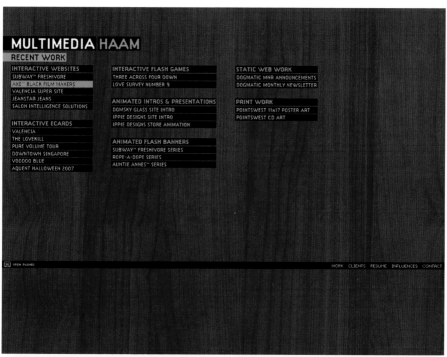

Info

DESIGN STUDIO: multimediaHAAM <www.multimediahaam.com>. /// **DESIGN:** Aragorn Ligocki. /// **PROGRAMMING:** Aragorn Ligocki. /// **CONTENTS:** Video, illustration, animation, photo, text. /// **TYPE:** Multimedia design and development. /// **TOOLS:** Flash, ActionScript, Sorenson Squeeze. /// **AWARDS:** DOPE Awards.

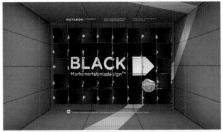

info

DESIGN STUDIO: SuperReal <www.superreal.de>. /// **DESIGN:** Oliver Cloppenburg (Creative Director/Art Director); Michael Wagner, Jörg Lehmann (Art Director). /// **PROGRAMMING:** Hannes Hoess, Jörg Lehmann. /// **CONTENTS:** Video, illustration, animation, photo, text. /// **TYPE:** Creative agency. /// **CLIENT:** Mutabor Design GmbH. /// **TOOLS:** Flash, Illustrator, Photoshop, Eclipse/FDT 3, PHP/MySQL, PureMVC, Papervision 3d, SWFAddress, After Effects. /// **COST:** 1130 hours.

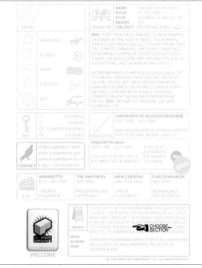

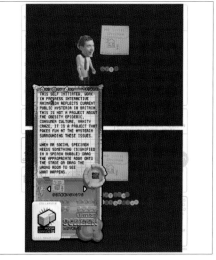

Info — DESIGN STUDIO: My Poor Brain <www.mypoorbrain.com>. /// DESIGN: Tim Smith. /// PROGRAMMING: Tim Smith. /// CONTENTS: illustration, animation, motion-graphics, photo. /// TYPE: Creative Agency. /// TOOLS: Illustrator, Photoshop, HTML, Flash, Action Script. /// COST: 150 hours.

NANOZOOM

www.nanozoom.net

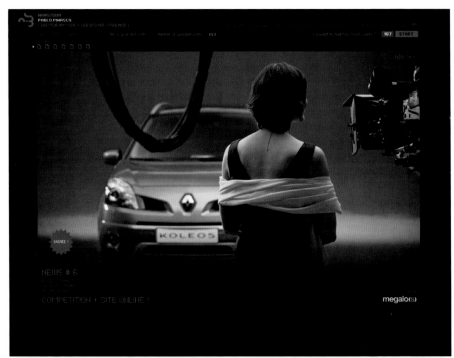

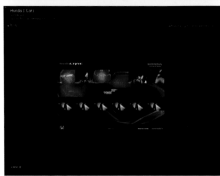
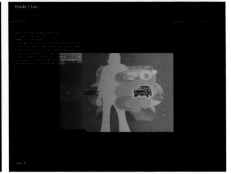

Info

DESIGN STUDIO: nanozoom <www.nanozoom.net>. /// **DESIGN:** Pablo Pinasco. /// **PROGRAMMING:** Pablo Pinasco. /// **CONTENTS:** Photo, illustration, text. /// **TYPE:** Art director and web designer. /// **TOOLS:** Flash, Fireworks, Photoshop, Dreamweaver.

Info

DESIGN STUDIO: Loyal Design <www.thisisloyal.com>. /// **DESIGN:** Loyal Design; National Television. /// **PROGRAMMING:** Loyal Design. /// **CONTENTS:**
Illustration, animation, motion-graphics, music, photo. /// **TYPE:** Art directors and designers. /// **CLIENT:** National Television. /// **TOOLS:** Photoshop,
Flash, HTML, PHP. /// **AWARDS:** FWA (Site of the Day). /// **COST:** 540 hours.

NAYEF FRANCIS

www.nayeffrancis.com

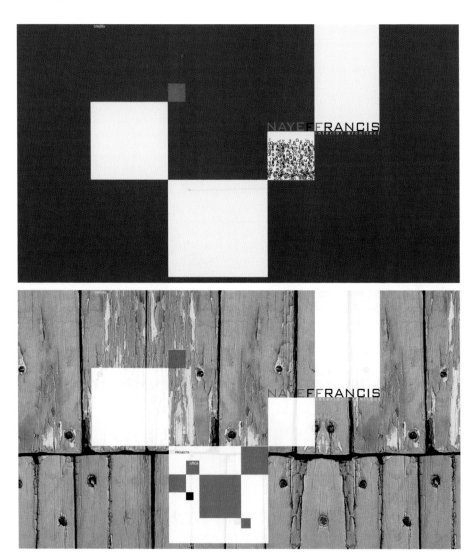

Info

DESIGN STUDIO: Nobrand <www.nobrand.name>. /// DESIGN: Badeeh Abla (Art Director); Enas Mtaweh (Junior Designer). /// PROGRAMMING: Rabeeh Abla (Software Architect); Saleem Badreddine (Junior Programmer). /// CONTENTS: Photo, text. /// TYPE: Interior designer. /// CLIENT: Nayef Francis. /// TOOLS: XML, PHP, Flash, Photoshop. /// COST: 120 hours.

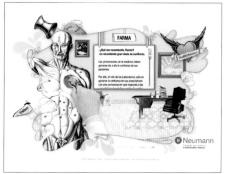

Info

DESIGN STUDIO: OnClick Studio <www.onclick.es>. /// **DESIGN:** Ramon del Nozal, Iosu Luengo, Alex Albizu. /// **PROGRAMMING:** Ramon del Nozal, Iosu Luengo, Alex Albizu. /// **CONTENTS:** Photo, illustration, text. /// **TYPE:** Health and wellness communication agency. /// **CLIENT:** Neumann Communication Agency. /// **TOOLS:** Flash, Photoshop, Illustrator, Php, MySQL, XML, After Effects, Audition. /// **COST:** 340 hours.

Info

DESIGN STUDIO: T-sign Studios <www.t-sign.com>. /// **DESIGN:** Jochen Repolust. /// **PROGRAMMING:** Robert Reich. /// **CONTENTS:** Video, photo, text. /// **TYPE:** Entertainment, visual effects production company. /// **CLIENT:** New Deal Studio. /// **TOOLS:** Photoshop, Flash, HTML, JavaScript, PHP. /// **AWARDS:** FWA. /// **COST:** 300 hours.

Info

DESIGN STUDIO: Mkt Virtual <www.mktvirtual.com.br>. /// DESIGN: Ludmilla Rossi. /// PROGRAMMING: Danilo Costa, Mauro de Tarso. /// CONTENTS: Photo, text. /// TYPE: Interior designer. /// CLIENT: Objeto de Desejo. /// TOOLS: Flash, XML, PHP. /// COST: 190 hours.

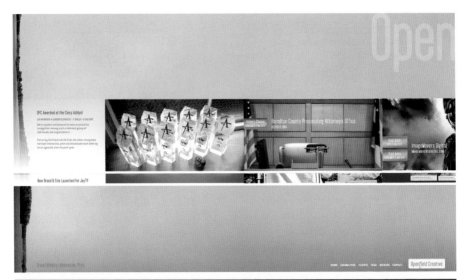

DESIGN STUDIO: Openfield Creative <www.openfieldcreative.com>. /// **DESIGN:** Brandon Blangger, Brian Keenan (Creative Direction); Josh Barnes (Strategy Director). /// **CONTENTS:** Photo, illustration, text. /// **TYPE:** Brand identity, interactive and print design studio. /// **TOOLS:** Flash, AS2, XML, Photoshop. /// **COST:** 125 hours.

OPTIKER KRAUSS

www.optikerkrauss.de

Info

DESIGN STUDIO: n-load <www.n-load.com>. /// **DESIGN:** Clemens Conrad, Sven Schneider. /// **PROGRAMMING:** Holger Fitzner. /// **CONTENTS:** Illustration, photo, music, animation. /// **TYPE:** Sun glasses company. /// **CLIENT:** Optiker Krauss GmbH. /// **TOOLS:** Photoshop, Illustrator, Dreamweaver, Flash, Scite, Flashdevelop. /// **COST:** 2 months.

Info

DESIGN STUDIO: mediaBOOM <www.mediaBOOM.com>. /// **DESIGN:** mediaBOOM. /// **PROGRAMMING:** mediaBOOM. /// **CONTENTS:** Illustration, animation, motion-graphics, music, photo, text. /// **TYPE:** Fashion company. /// **CLIENT:** Prospect Denim. /// **TOOLS:** Flash, HTML, Photoshop, After Effects, Maya. /// **AWARDS:** Webby Awards, FWA (Site of the Day), Connecticut Art Directors Club (Best in Show). /// **COST:** 400 hours.

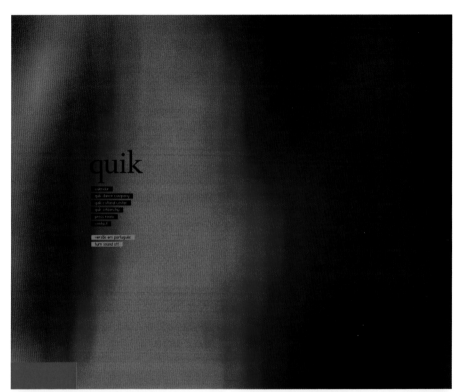

Info

DESIGN STUDIO: Osso <www.osso.com.br>. /// **DESIGN:** Fred Paulino (Art Direction/Concept); Paulo Barcelos (Design); Laura Barbi (Project Manager). /// **PROGRAMMING:** Fred Paulino, Paulo Barcelos, Julião Villas. /// **CONTENTS:** Photo, text. /// **TYPE:** Dance company. /// **CLIENT:** Rodrigo Quik, Letícia Carneiro. /// **TOOLS:** XML, Flash, Photoshop. /// **COST:** 240 hours.

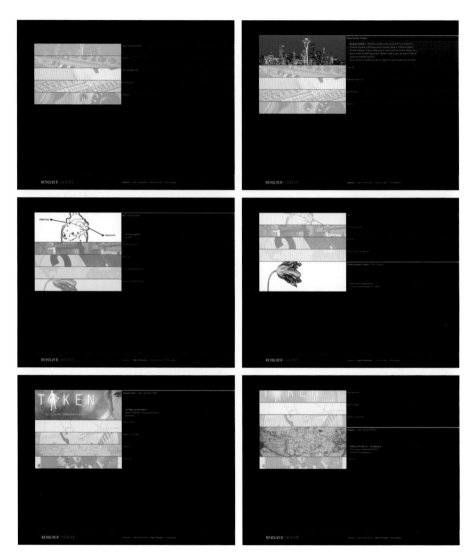

Info

DESIGN STUDIO: Revolver Creative <www.revolvercreative.com>. /// **DESIGN:** Matthew Fordham. /// **PROGRAMMING:** Matthew Fordham. ///
CONTENTS: Music, photo, text. /// **TYPE:** Interactive and music production company. /// **TOOLS:** Flash, Photoshop, XML. /// **COST:** 40 hours.

ADVERTISING

Info

DESIGN STUDIO: Hello Monday <www.hellomonday.com>. /// **DESIGN:** Hello Monday; Designbolaget. /// **PROGRAMMING:** Hello Monday. /// **CONTENTS:** Photo. /// **TYPE:** Photographer. /// **CLIENT:** Robin Skjoldborg. /// **TOOLS:** Flash, Flex, XML, PHP, Photoshop. /// **AWARDS:** NewWebPick, Website Design Awards. /// **COST:** 120 hours.

NEW WORK1 / Three 6 Mafia ·Karl Kani ·Ciapponi Studio

EDITORIAL5 / Man Magazine

ADVERTISING7 / Guru Denim / Agency . Pirates

Info

DESIGN STUDIO: DC <www.dcworks.nl>. /// **DESIGN:** Maarten Mieras. /// **PROGRAMMING:** Michiel Sikma. /// **CONTENTS:** Photo. /// **TYPE:** Photographer. /// **CLIENT:** Ruud Baan. /// **TOOLS:** Flash, XML. /// **COST:** 100 hours.

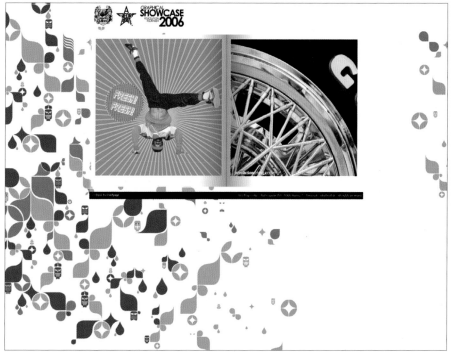

Info

DESIGN STUDIO: Hello Monday <www.hellomonday.com>. /// **DESIGN:** Hello Monday. /// **PROGRAMMING:** Hello Monday. /// **CONTENTS:** Photo, illustration, text. /// **TYPE:** Fashion designer. /// **CLIENT:** Robin Skjoldborg. /// **TOOLS:** Flash, Flex, XML, PHP, Photoshop. /// **COST:** 125 hours.

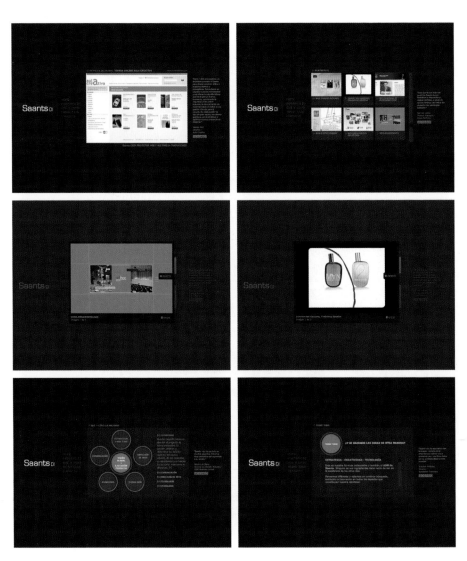

DESIGN STUDIO: Saants DI <www.saants.es>. /// **DESIGN:** Ibon Fernandez de Landa, Anna Llobet. /// **PROGRAMMING:** Francisco Gutiérrez. /// **CONTENTS:** Photo, illustration, text. /// **TYPE:** Interactive agency. /// **CLIENT:** Saants DI. /// **TOOLS:** ASP.net, Saants CMS, Web Developer. /// **COST:** 240 hours.

Info

DESIGN STUDIO: Mkt Virtual <www.mktvirtual.com.br>. /// **DESIGN:** Ludmilla Rossi. /// **PROGRAMMING:** Fabio Paes Pedro. /// **CONTENTS:** Illustration, motion-graphics, photo, text. /// **TYPE:** Video and motion design company. /// **CLIENT:** Santa Produtora. /// **TOOLS:** Flash, XML, PHP. /// **COST:** 180 hours.

Info

DESIGN STUDIO: DrawingArt <www.drawingart.org>. /// **DESIGN:** Miro Koljanin. /// **PROGRAMMING:** Miro Koljanin. /// **CONTENTS:** Photo, text. /// **TYPE:** Photographer. /// **CLIENT:** Saso Kos. /// **TOOLS:** Photoshop, Flash, XML, HTML, PHP. /// **AWARDS:** FWA (Site of the Day), OOPE Awards, The Dreamer, Fcukstar.

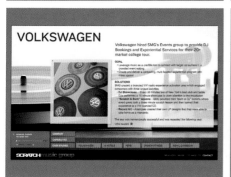

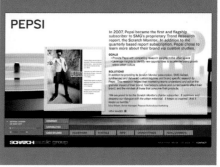

DESIGN STUDIO: The Killswitch Collective <www.killswitchcollective.com>. /// **DESIGN:** Lindsey Turner (Senior Designer); Meredith Martin (Creative Director). /// **CONTENTS:** Music, photo, text. /// **TYPE:** Music consulting group. /// **CLIENT:** Scratch Music Group. /// **TOOLS:** XML, HTML, Photoshop, Flash. /// **COST:** 120 hours.

Info

DESIGN STUDIO: Strange <www.strangecorp.com>. /// **DESIGN:** Jamie Sergeant, Lee Poynter, Nick Bain. /// **PROGRAMMING:** Ricardo Sanchez, John Parker. /// **CONTENTS:** Photo. /// **TYPE:** Fashion designers. /// **CLIENT:** Secret Circus. /// **TOOLS:** Illustrator, Photoshop, Flash, PHP, XML, HTML. /// **COST:** 200 hours.

DESIGN STUDIO: SectionSeven <www.sectionseven.com>. /// **DESIGN:** Craig Erickson. /// **PROGRAMMING:** Jason Keimig. /// **CONTENTS:** Illustration, photo, text. /// **TYPE:** Interactive design studio. /// **TOOLS:** Adobe CS2, ActionScript, XML. /// **AWARDS:** FWA (Site of the Day/Top 50), Communication Arts Interactive Design, Seattle Show (Gold).

Info

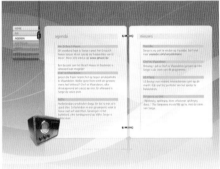

Info

DESIGN STUDIO: Weblounge <www.weblounge.be>. /// **DESIGN:** Kristof van Rentergem. /// **PROGRAMMING:** Kristof van Rentergem, Maarten Bulckaen. /// **CONTENTS:** Music, photo, text. /// **TYPE:** Radiohost. /// **CLIENT:** Serge de Marre. /// **TOOLS:** Flash, Photoshop. /// **AWARDS:** American Design Award, Flashloaded. /// **COST:** 80 hours.

Info

DESIGN STUDIO: Sir Patroclo <www.sir-patroclo.com>. /// **DESIGN:** Patricio Berríos Lobos. /// **PROGRAMMING:** Patricio Berríos Lobos. /// **CONTENTS:** Illustration, animation, motion-graphics, photo, text. /// **TYPE:** Creative Agency. /// **TOOLS:** Flash, HTML, PHP. /// **AWARDS:** FWA (Site of the Day), NewWebPick, Website Design Awards, DOPE Awards (Professional), American Design Awards (Platinum), Smashing Magazine. /// **COST:** 240 hours.

Info

DESIGN STUDIO: Skaffs <www.skaffs.com>. /// **DESIGN:** Skaffs: Luke Feldman. /// **PROGRAMMING:** Skaffs: Luke Feldman. /// **CONTENTS:** Illustration, animation, motion-graphics, photo, text. /// **TYPE:** Creative Agency. /// **TOOLS:** Flash, Illustrator, Photoshop, XML, HTML, CSS. /// **AWARDS:** The Best Designs.com, My Design Award (Voted Top Designs), Faves.com, All Things Kawaii (Voted Top 10). /// **COST:** 30 hours.

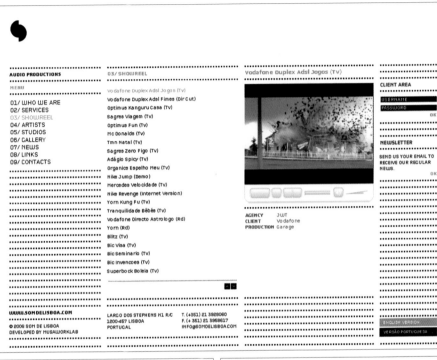

Info

DESIGN STUDIO: Musa WorkLab <www.musaworklab.com>. /// **DESIGN:** Musa WorkLab. /// **PROGRAMMING:** Micael Monteiro. /// **CONTENTS:** Music, video, photo, text. /// **TYPE:** Sound design and production. /// **CLIENT:** Som de Lisboa. /// **TOOLS:** Flash, Photoshop, FreeHand, Quicktime Pro, PHP. /// **COST:** 300 hours.

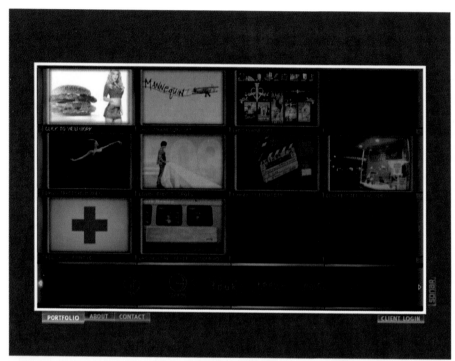

Info

DESIGN STUDIO: Sonar <www.sonarproductions.com>. /// **DESIGN:** Wayne Robins (Creative Director); Jake Mikosh (Copy); Nick Kaye (Graphic Design/Animation). /// **PROGRAMMING:** Greg Schomburg (Flash/XML); Aram Zadikian (Flash). /// **CONTENTS:** Photo, illustration, animation, video, motion-graphics, text. /// **TYPE:** Designer and art director. /// **CLIENT:** Wayne Robins. /// **TOOLS:** Flash, XML, Final Cut Pro, 3d Studio Max, After Effects, Photoshop, Illustrator. /// **AWARDS:** NewWebPick, favorstar.com, sj63.com, Page Crush, gouw.nu, Xhilarate. /// **COST:** 240 hours.

Info

DESIGN STUDIO: Square Circle Media <www.sqcircle.com>. /// **DESIGN:** Danny Burnside, Adam Pilarski, Stella Jordan. /// **PROGRAMMING:** George Medve, Chris Sees. /// **CONTENTS:** Photo, text. /// **TYPE:** Media agency. /// **TOOLS:** Flash, Eclipse, Cinema 4D, Photoshop, PHPeclipse (Eclipse plug-in), After Effects. /// **AWARDS:** FWA (Site of the Day), Creative Website Awards (Site of the Year), Web Design Index 7, DOPE Awards, ADS Editor's choice.

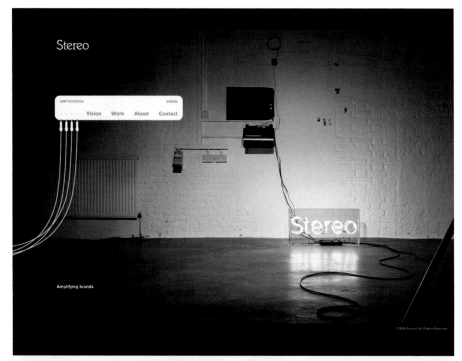

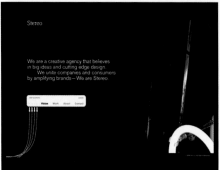

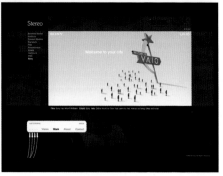

Info

DESIGN STUDIO: Stereo <www.hellostereo.co.uk>. /// **DESIGN:** Stereo. /// **PROGRAMMING:** Stereo. /// **CONTENTS:** Animation, text, illustration, photo. /// **TYPE:** Agency. /// **TOOLS:** Illustrator, Photoshop, After Effects, Flash, HTML, Wordpress PHP 4, JavaScript. /// **COST:** 2500 hours.

STEREONOISE

www.stereo-noise.com

DESIGN STUDIO: Aer visual studio <www.aerstudio.com>. /// **DESIGN:** Aer studio. /// **PROGRAMMING:** Aer studio. /// **CONTENTS:** Video, illustration, animation, photo, text. /// **TYPE:** Inventor. /// **CLIENT:** Stereonoise. /// **TOOLS:** Flash, XML, HTML, PHP, MySQL, Illustrator. /// **AWARDS:** ADG-FAD Laus Awards. /// **COST:** 360 hours.

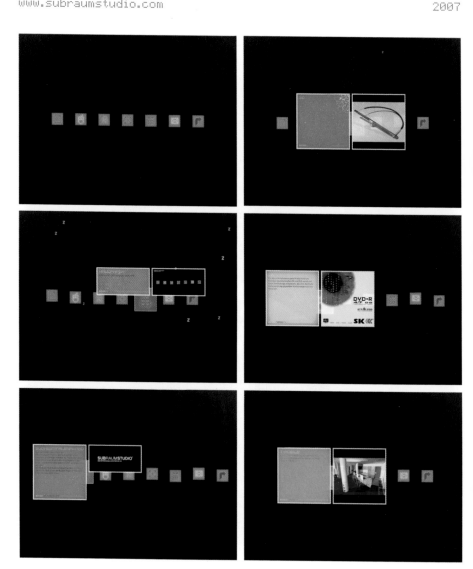

DESIGN STUDIO: Nalindesign <www.nalindesign.com>. /// **DESIGN:** Andre Weier. /// **PROGRAMMING:** Andre Weier. /// **CONTENTS:** Photo, illustration, text. /// **TYPE:** Industrial design and architecture studio. /// **CLIENT:** Subraumstudio. /// **TOOLS:** Flash, Photoshop, HTML, PHP, CSS, Javascript, htaccess, Effective CMS. /// **AWARDS:** American Design Award (Gold), Südwestfalenaward (Best Experimental Website), CoolHomepages (Site of the Week), Creative Website Awards. /// **COST:** 3 months.

TAKAKI KUMADA

www.takaki-kumada.com

Info

DESIGN STUDIO: Simone Inc. <www.ilovesimone.com>. /// DESIGN: Kaie Murakami (Art Direction); Hiroyuki Misono. /// PROGRAMMING: Hiroyuki Misono. /// CONTENTS: Photo, text. /// TYPE: Photographer. /// CLIENT: Takaki Kumada. /// TOOLS: Flash, XML. /// COST: 50 hours.

DESIGN STUDIO: Grand Creative <www.wearegrand.com>. /// **DESIGN:** Luke Canning. /// **PROGRAMMING:** Matthew Quinn. /// **CONTENTS:** Video, illustration, animation, photo, text. /// **TYPE:** Creative Agency. /// **CLIENT:** TBWA\Toronto. /// **TOOLS:** Photoshop, Illustrator, Flash, Coda, Transmit. /// **AWARDS:** ADCC, Applied Arts.

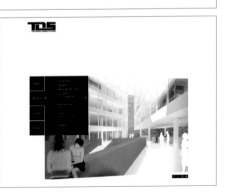

Info

DESIGN STUDIO: Pixel <www.pixel.ge>. /// **DESIGN:** George Khmaladze. /// **PROGRAMMING:** George Marnadze. /// **CONTENTS:** Photo, text. ///
TYPE: Architecture company. /// **CLIENT:** TDS – Technical Design Studio. /// **TOOLS:** Flash, XML. /// **COST:** 1 month.

DESIGN STUDIO: Openfield Creative <www.openfieldcreative.com>. /// **DESIGN:** Brandon Blangger, Brian Keenan (Creative Direction); Josh Barnes (Strategy Director); Matt Broerman (Design Director). /// **PROGRAMMING:** Matt Broerman. /// **CONTENTS:** Photo, text. /// **TYPE:** Photography studio. **CLIENT:** Teri Studios. /// **TOOLS:** Flash, AS2, XML, Photoshop. /// **COST:** 130 hours.

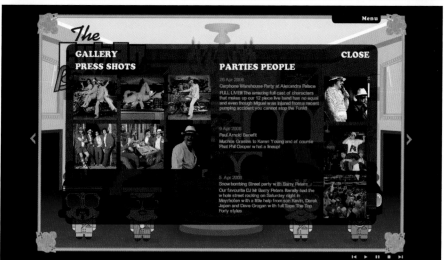

Info

DESIGN STUDIO: Clusta Ltd <www.clusta.com>. /// DESIGN: Martin Donnelly. /// PROGRAMMING: Sean Duffy. /// CONTENTS: Photo, music, animation, illustration, text. /// TYPE: Music and comedy act. /// CLIENT: The Cuban Brothers. /// TOOLS: Flash, ActionScript, XML, ASP.net.

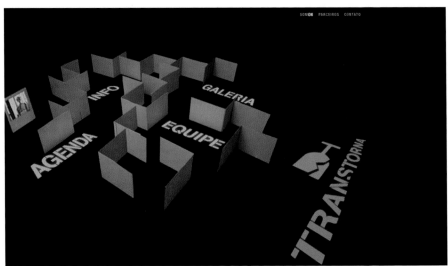

Info

DESIGN STUDIO: Osso <www.osso.com.br>. /// **DESIGN:** Fred Paulino (Art Director/Concept); João Henrique Wilbert, Julião Villas, Alexandre B. (Design); Laura Barbi (Project Manager). /// **PROGRAMMING:** Fred Paulino, João Henrique Wilbert, Julião Villas. /// **CONTENTS:** Illustration, photo, text. /// **TYPE:** Dance company. /// **CLIENT:** Companhia de Dança Palácio das Artes. /// **TOOLS:** Flash, Photoshop. /// **COST:** 120 hours.

Info

DESIGN STUDIO: Loyal Design <www.thisisloyal.com>. /// **DESIGN:** Loyal Design. /// **PROGRAMMING:** Loyal Design. /// **CONTENTS:** Illustration, animation, motion-graphics, video, photo, text. /// **TYPE:** Designers and art directors. /// **CLIENT:** Troika. /// **TOOLS:** Photoshop, Flash, HTML, PHP. /// **COST:** 500 hours.

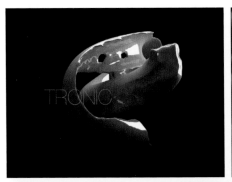

Info

DESIGN STUDIO: Tronic Studio <www.tronicstudio.com>. /// **DESIGN:** Vivian Rosenthal, Jessi Seppi, Rei Inamoto. /// **PROGRAMMING:** Rei Inamoto. ///
CONTENTS: Motion-graphics, video, photo, text. /// **TYPE:** Design studio. /// **TOOLS:** Flash.

Info

DESIGN STUDIO: Bubble <www.thebubblesite.co.uk>. /// **DESIGN:** James Gilbert, Mark Atherley, Angela Roche. /// **PROGRAMMING:** Paul Aspden. /// **CONTENTS:** Animation, photo, video, text. /// **TYPE:** Creative Agency. /// **CLIENT:** Uniform. /// **TOOLS:** Illustrator, Photoshop, Flash, ActionScript, Dreamweaver, XML, HTML, PHP. /// **AWARDS:** Silver Roses Award. /// **COST:** 100 hours.

Info

DESIGN STUDIO: Medusateam <www.medusateam.com>. /// **DESIGN:** Medusateam. /// **PROGRAMMING:** Medusateam. /// **CONTENTS:** Illustration, animation, photo, text. /// **TYPE:** Design Agency. /// **CLIENT:** Urbansoldierz. /// **TOOLS:** Flash, Photoshop, Illustrator, XML, HTML, PHP/MySQL. /// **COST:** 350 hours.

DESIGN STUDIO: VaryWell <www.varywell.com>. /// **DESIGN:** Ryan Hickner. /// **PROGRAMMING:** Jason Hickner. /// **CONTENTS:** Video, illustration, photo, text. /// **TYPE:** Creative Agency. /// **TOOLS:** Flash, Papervision 3d. /// **AWARDS:** FWA, DOPE Awards, Creative Website Awards, NewWebPick, MyDesignAward, Website Design Awards. /// **COST:** 3 months.

Info

VENENO

www.venenoinc.com

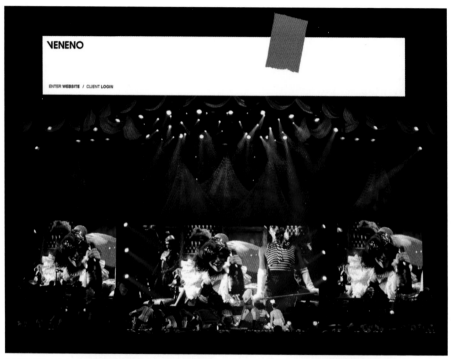

Info

DESIGN STUDIO: Loyal Design <www.thisisloyal.com>. /// **DESIGN:** Loyal Design. /// **PROGRAMMING:** Loyal Design. /// **CONTENTS:** Video, music, photo, text. /// **TYPE:** Art director and producer. /// **CLIENT:** Veneno Inc. /// **TOOLS:** Photoshop, Flash, HTML, PHP. /// **COST:** 490 hours.

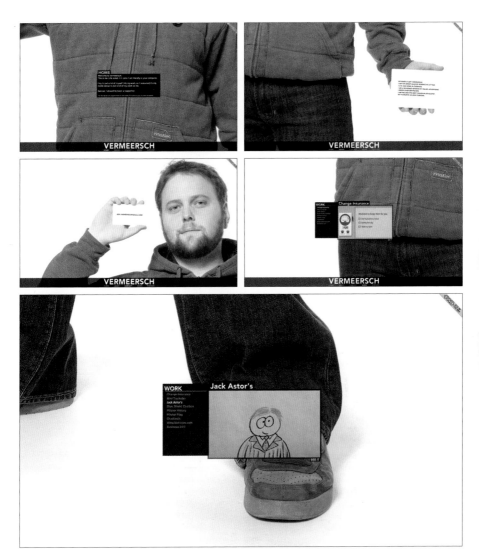

Info

Design Studio: Vermeersch <www.vermeersch.ca>. /// **Design:** Jeff Vermeersch; Finn O'Hara (Photo); Sasha Moroz (Additional Design). ///
Programming: Jeff Vermeersch. /// **Contents:** Illustration, photo, text. /// **Type:** Flash designer. /// **Tools:** Flash, Photoshop, Leaf Capture. ///
Awards: FWA (Site of the Day), FITC (Best Canadian Developer), DOPE Awards. /// **Cost:** 60 hours.

VINCENT VELLA

www.vincent-vella.com

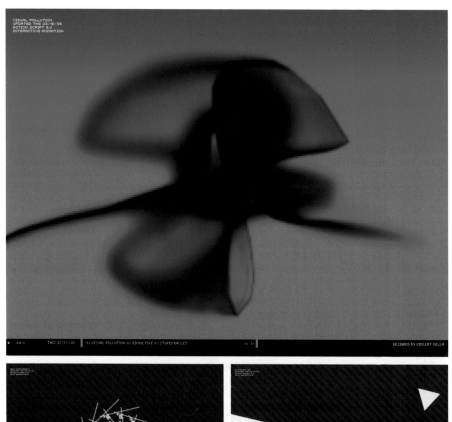

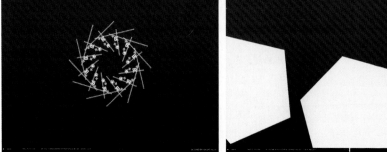

Info

DESIGN STUDIO: Vincent Vella <www.vincent-vella.com>. /// **DESIGN:** Vincent Vella. /// **PROGRAMMING:** Vincent Vella. /// **CONTENTS:** Motion-graphics, video, photo, text. /// **TYPE:** Creative Director. /// **TOOLS:** Flash. /// **AWARDS:** DesignCharts, Strange Fruits, Website Design Award. /// **COST:** 2 months.

Info

DESIGN STUDIO: DrawingArt <www.drawingart.org>. /// **DESIGN:** Miro Koljanin. /// **PROGRAMMING:** Miro Koljanin. /// **CONTENTS:** Video, illustration, photo, text. /// **TYPE:** Digital artist. /// **CLIENT:** Virtual Murder. /// **TOOLS:** Photoshop, Flash, XML, HTML, PHP. /// **AWARDS:** Faveup, Design Snack, Website Design Awards, Netinspiration, e-Creative, The Dreamer.

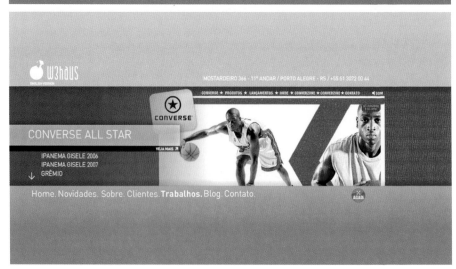

DESIGN STUDIO: W3Haus <www.w3haus.com.br>. /// **DESIGN:** Rodrigo Cauduro. /// **PROGRAMMING:** Alessandro Cauduro, Luiz Ricardo Sordi. /// **CONTENTS:** Illustration, video, photo, text. /// **TYPE:** Interactive agency. /// **TOOLS:** Photoshop, Flash, HTML. /// **COST:** 400 hours.

Info

Design Studio: DC <www.dcworks.nl>. /// **Design:** Maarten Mieras, Martijn Rietveld. /// **Programming:** Michiel Sikma. /// **Contents:** Photo, text. /// **Type:** Standup comedian. /// **Client:** Howard Komproe. /// **Tools:** Flash, XML. /// **Cost:** 200 hours.

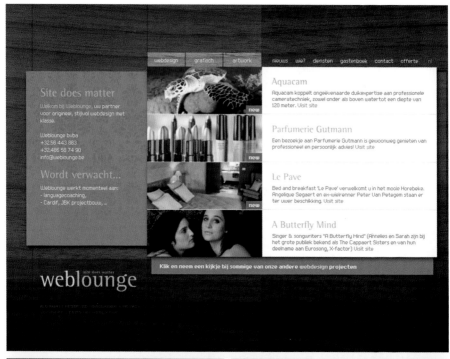

DESIGN STUDIO: Weblounge <www.weblounge.be>. /// DESIGN: Kristof van Rentergem. /// PROGRAMMING: Kristof van Rentergem, Maarten Bulckaen. /// CONTENTS: Photo, illustration, text. /// TYPE: Interactive agency. /// TOOLS: Photoshop, Flash. /// AWARDS: Webmaster Award, Mowsnet (Bronze), CoolHomepages, The Best Designs.com, Page Crush, Web Creme, Designcollector, iStockphoto, Design Shack, Xhilarate. /// COST: 140 hours.

Info

DESIGN STUDIO: WHITEvoid interactive art & design <www.whitevoid.com>. /// **DESIGN:** Christopher Bauder, Andre Stubbe. /// **PROGRAMMING:** Andre Stubbe, Markus Lerner. /// **CONTENTS:** Video, illustration, photo, text. /// **TYPE:** Interactive agency. /// **TOOLS:** Photoshop, Illustrator, Flash (ActionScript), Papervision 3d. /// **AWARDS:** FWA (Site of the Day), Website Design Awards, Interactive Media Awards, Design Licks, Hotwebber.

Info

DESIGN STUDIO: Musa WorkLab <www.musaworklab.com>. /// **DESIGN:** Musa WorkLab. /// **PROGRAMMING:** Musa WorkLab. /// **CONTENTS:** Photo, text. /// **TYPE:** Communication, public relations and fashion event production. /// **CLIENT:** XN Brand Dynamics. /// **TOOLS:** Flash, Photoshop, FreeHand, HTML, Quicktime Pro. /// **COST:** 400 hours.

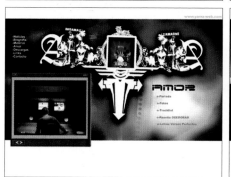

DESIGN STUDIO: YAMA <www.yama-web.com>. /// **DESIGN:** Eduardo Rodriguez Perez. /// **PROGRAMMING:** Juan Paredes Correro. /// **CONTENTS:** Music, video, text, illustration, photo. /// **TYPE:** Musician. /// **CLIENT:** Tuning Records. /// **TOOLS:** Flash, Dreamweaver, Photoshop. /// **COST:** 30 hours.

Info

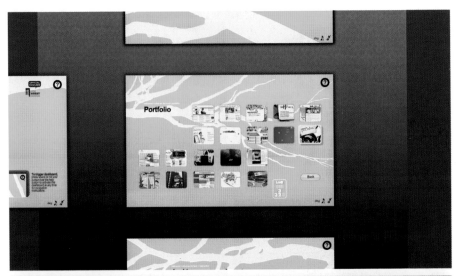

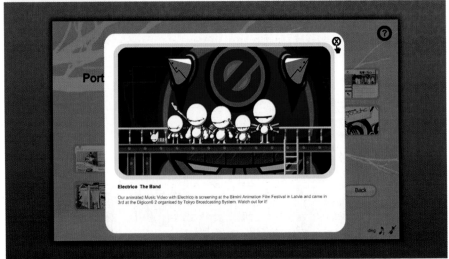

Info

DESIGN STUDIO: yolk <www.yolk.com.sg>. /// **DESIGN:** Low Jun Jek, Kelveen Soh, Shante Lee, Michelle Tan, Wu Wanni. /// **PROGRAMMING:** Wu Wanni, Jamie Lim. /// **CONTENTS:** Illustration, animation, photo, text. /// **TYPE:** Digital media agency. /// **CLIENT:** yolk. /// **TOOLS:** Flash, Photoshop, ASP, HTML. /// **AWARDS:** Webby Awards (Nominee), FWA (Site of the Day), Asia Interactive Awards. /// **COST:** 2 weeks.

Info

DESIGN STUDIO: Zero Style <http://0-style.com>. /// **DESIGN:** Joshua Stearns. /// **PROGRAMMING:** Joshua Stearns. /// **CONTENTS:** Video, motion-graphics, photo, text. /// **TYPE:** Interactive design studio. /// **TOOLS:** Flash, Photoshop, After Effects, Premiere. /// **AWARDS:** FWA (Site of the Day), DOPE Awards (Professional), Creative Website Awards (Site of the Day), Mowsnet (Bronze), e-Creative (Site of the Day), Design Licks (Site of the Day). /// **COST:** 160 hours.

Dear readers, here is the second volume on portfolios online, but not a revised edition. They are all new. This book is a continuation of the First Web Design: Portfolios book, published about three years ago, but this time focusing on showcases built using Flash. It has once more been a hard time deciding which offices we would have to leave out, especially with making a choice amongst websites from the creative industry, which these days are the only addresses that really matter. The internet is not only becoming bigger, it is becoming better. The quality of the work and the availability of resources are now reaching a point where creators have almost all the freedom they always hoped to have. It is of course also becoming more complex at the same time, as designers and corporations push the available resources to their limits, demanding a whole new way of thinking for the web.

Portfolios online now require briefing and strategy discussions, a conceptual development phase, video production, special shooting sections, special effects, soundtrack, illustration, customised content management, and so on. It is unprecedented. This book is intended to serve as a reference for anyone wishing to work in this area at the highest levels online. Today such portfolios are almost a necessity for any business or professional. The portfolios of the featured studios, the complexity of the work they carry out, and the demanding clients they handle, will leave no doubt that the works in this book are a reference for some of the best work seen recently.

We have had the good fortune to work with great contributors in producing this book, starting with Steve Le Marquand, from Resn, in New Zealand, on the importance of digital portfolios. The second case study is by Myles McGuinness, who has written about the redesign of his own portfolio, 9Myles. The next is by Jason Stone, from mimeArtist, who produces cutting-edge flash sites, but has opted to go for a low-profile, yet very effective online showcase of his start-up design studio. The fourth case is by the team of Postgal Workshop, a leading agency in Hong Kong, on the state of creative portfolios in Asia. Apart from these, we have had the pleasure to receive tons of submissions from the creative design-workers active in this digital area.

Also special thanks as ever to Daniel Siciliano Brêtas for making the whole process move so smoothly, and to our production man Stefan Klatte for making this series continue to look more attractive with each new book, and for his ability to work at such high speeds.

Enjoy the new selection of online portfolios here!

Julius Wiedemann